given in memory
of
Carolyn Tsimortos
a friend who loved
life, books and horses.

TRAINING YOUR COLT
TO·RIDE·AND·DRIVE

Happiness is a filly of your own to develop.

TRAINING YOUR COLT
TO·RIDE·AND·DRIVE

A Complete Guide for Pleasure or Show

MARILYN C. CHILDS and
RICK M. WALLEN

Trafalgar Square Publishing
NORTH POMFRET, VERMONT

Revised edition published in 1993 by
Trafalgar Square Publishing
North Pomfret, Vermont 05053

The authors have made every effort to obtain permission for all photographs used in this book. In some cases, however, the photographers were not known and therefore are not identified. Should any names become available, the photographers will be credited in future editions, assuming permission is granted.

Disclaimer of Liability:
The Authors and Publisher shall have neither liability nor responsibility to any person or entity with respect to any loss or damage caused or alleged to be caused directly or indirectly by the information contained in this book. While the book is as accurate as the Authors can make it, there may be errors, omissions, and inaccuracies. ·

Library of Congress Cataloging-in-Publication Data

Childs, Marilyn Carlson.
    Training your colt to ride and drive : a complete guide for pleasure or show / by Marilyn C. Childs and Rick M. Wallen. — Rev. ed.
      p. cm.
    Includes index.
    ISBN 0-943955-83-1
      1. Horses—Training.   I. Wallen, Rick M. II. Title.
SF287.C52 1993
636.1'088—dc20   93-28286
                      CIP

ISBN: 0-943955-83-1
Printed in the United States of America
10 9 8 7 6 5 4 3 2 1

Dedicated to
Harold L. Childs
and
Marilyn J. Wallen

ACKNOWLEDGMENTS

The authors' special thanks are due to Betsy Melvin, Ann Mac-Murray Cox, and Chris and Leon Roberts, who provided many of the photographs used in the training sequences. We are grateful to Polly Holm, Bruce and Rusty Rademan, the late Dr. Frances Schaeffer, the late George Huss, and the Teater family for providing photographs of show champions.

The book would not be complete without the cooperation of many who helped with illustrations; we wish to acknowledge the following people whose photographs are unidentified in the book: George Robertson, Martin and Roberto Gonzalez, John Warner, Linda Gauthier, Perry Pereand, Cindy Koch, Harold Childs, Cheryl Dixon, Cherie Ort, and Sarah Birmingham.

Lastly, it has been particularly gratifying to work with Caroline Robbins, publisher, and Martha Cook, editor, whose understanding and love of horses led them to devote extra time to challenge us constantly to sharpen the focus of this book for the amateur reader.

CONTENTS

———•———

INTRODUCTION

———•———

This book has been written for the countless amateur horse owners who undertake, through necessity or choice, to break and train their own horses.* To try to put between the covers of a single book everything one should know in order to produce a reliable pleasure or show horse is perhaps an impossible task, for a book is a poor substitute for personal instruction and experience. Nonetheless, these amateur owners, who are actually the lifeblood of the sport, do need guidance, even though they cannot afford to devote years, or even months, to learning the necessary techniques. The printed word can often lead them toward solutions that would take a long time to discover through trial and error.

Some amateurs, of course, should never attempt to train their own horses. Complete beginners or people of frail constitution, timid temperament, or limited patience are hardly likely to succeed. However, in practice this kind of person rarely makes the attempt and hardly ever perseveres in it. For the amateur who rides fairly well, and who is willing to apply some intelligence, determination, and patience to the job, training the horse is a far from impossible task and an extraordinarily rewarding one.

*The reader who has not yet acquired his colt or horse to train is advised to read Chapter 10 first.

1

It is almost better not to train at all than to train badly. The common-sense approach to horses demands that the handler stay one step ahead of the animal mentally. Our aim is to teach the colt only the right conduct, and to reward it. To prevent trouble before it starts is wisdom; the colt or horse that has never learned to do anything wrong will delight his owners and handlers throughout his life. Undoing or correcting bad habits is a challenge for even the most expert professionals in the field, and the professional horseman is the first to admit that there may be no solution for the problem horse that has gotten badly out of hand.

Certainly there are many ways of training horses, but the methods suggested here in chapter 1 through chapter 4, and chapters 9 and 10, will reflect principles that may, with little modification, be applied to almost any breed of horse, whether it is used as a sport horse or a show horse. We define a sport horse as any horse used for riding and driving activities such as dressage, eventing, hunting, trail riding, or carriage driving. A show horse, for which the remainder of the book is specifically written, we define as any horse ridden or driven under English tack or fine harness and expected to possess a high head carriage and high leg action as seen in the park and gaited divisions (and even in English pleasure classes to a certain degree). Many, but not all, Saddlebreds, Morgans, National Show Horses, Arabians, and Hackneys are shown in this manner.

We hope that those who own horses for their personal enjoyment and pleasure will benefit from the suggestions in this book. The training methods we teach are a condensation or simplification of the training routines used by the professionals, adapted for use by the amateur owner. But while professionals can spend years in perfecting a champion hunter, a thrilling five-gaited horse or a top roadster, the amateur will be more impatient to attain personal enjoyment from his colt. Accordingly, manners are the prime consideration for the amateur, rather than the flashy brilliance of the top show champions. Yet, just as nothing can match the work of the nation's best professional horsemen in their fields for the highest standard of performance, for human companionship and personal pride nothing can ever top the rapport between the man and mount that have "grown wise together."

AUTHORS' NOTE

———————•———————

Given the clear distinction today between the show ring and other horse sport activities we will use the terms *show horse* or *sport horse*, as defined in the introduction, throughout the book to clarify which group of horses we are speaking of when describing certain training techniques that apply to one group rather than the other.

CHAPTER 1

HALTER-BREAKING THE FOAL

No matter what a horse ultimately is to be used for, its education normally begins with halter-breaking. This is a simple process, especially if it is begun during the first few weeks while the foal is still with its dam; a foal that is only a few days old is not strong enough or coordinated enough to put up much of an argument. A week to ten days is a good time to start halter-breaking a foal. The foal can then be handled while it is still small and tractable, and a mutual confidence is developed through petting and playing which will form a good foundation for later training. Some people prefer to let the foal just grow and enjoy itself for about three weeks before bothering it with a halter. And though the foal at that age can put up a bit more of a battle, there are rarely any real problems unless the mare is unusually fussy.

It is best to start with the mare and foal together in the stall. Before entering, try to adjust the halter (we prefer a leather halter) to approximately the correct size for the foal. When you enter the stall, lead the mare over to a corner, and try to coax the foal in behind her, moving very slowly and deliberately. Try to approach the foal from the left, so that you can slip the halter on and buckle it from the same side. If the foal is gentle and will allow himself to be rubbed, you can take plenty of time scratching his back, his shoulder, and finally his neck. Many foals will relish this attention and be eager for more. Then it becomes merely a matter of steadily moving the caresses toward the head. The trick is to slip the halter over the nose so smoothly that the foal hardly realizes it is there, and then to slip the crownpiece over and buckle it without a fuss.

If the mare is excitable, the above procedure will be more easily said than done. Whenever trouble is anticipated, it is wise to be prepared with one or even two assistants before attempting the first haltering. Then one handler holds the mare across the corner of the stall and quiets her, perhaps diverting her attention with a few oats, while the second urges the foal up into the corner behind her, and either he or a third person squeezes in between the mare and foal, with the wall behind him, and slips the halter on the foal. Again, this procedure should be carried out with the greatest possible quiet and deliberation.

Once the halter is on, you must decide whether to continue handling the foal or leave him alone. This choice is determined largely by the age and attitude of the foal. If he is young and has been petted a lot, this is a good time to pet him a bit more while holding the halter. If the small foal tries to pull back and throw himself, the handler can stay with him, allowing him to regain his feet, and restore his confidence by further petting or scratching.

If the foal is pretty well grown, however, or has not had prior handling, or if the dam is nervous, it is best to move quietly away once the halter is on. The foal will shake it for a while, find that it stays on, and after a few days accept it as inevitable without associating it with force or fright. If you decide to leave the foal haltered, the stall should be thoroughly examined for any protruding objects on which the foal's halter could become tangled up or snagged.

The foal of three months or older is pretty well developed and strong if he has matured normally. If he has been handled since colthood, the difficulties of haltering should be slight and the approach can be the same as with a younger foal. However, if the colt was born in a herd and allowed to run until he was several months old, he may be quite wild and highly suspicious of a human's approach unless it is perfectly clear that the person is only bringing feed. The dam, too, may well be less quiet and gentle than a mare that has been handled and petted regularly. So it is necessary to have extra help for the handling of this foal the first time.

The mare and foal should be put in a box stall, one person holding the mare with her nose headed into a corner and her body diagonally placed to the wall. The second handler will have the halter ready; the third will herd the colt up into the corner between the mare and the wall. Probably the colt will be rearing and plunging, and it may only be possible for the handler to work in back of the foal, or between foal and mare. The person with the halter must stay on the left side of the mare, hoping to reach under her neck and slip the halter on quickly when the foal is herded into position.

Once the colt is driven up into the corner between the mare and wall, the herder behind him can grab the colt's tail close to the dock and raise it up over the colt's back. This must be done swiftly and requires boldness or experience, but it is the quickest and surest way to keep a colt in a fairly immobile position long enough for the handler to slip on the halter. Raising the tail and pushing it forward over the back works on the spinal muscles and tends to "freeze" the colt. With a good handler at the tail, it is possible to slip the halter on with little trouble and snap a lead shank to it. Continue holding the tail up long enough to allow some petting of this older, wilder colt.

If there has been a battle to get this older colt haltered, you may as well go a bit further and try to teach him that the halter is something that holds and restrains him. Once the tail is released, the colt will resist any effort to hold him. Attach a long lead shank and be prepared to see the colt buck, rear, and throw himself. Only the colt's handler and the person holding the mare should remain in the stall, for there will be a flurry of activity as the colt throws himself about and the handler tries to hang on to the lead. If the mare is quiet, the handler can use her as a pulley, allowing the foal to pull against her body. If she is not, it may be necessary for the third person to return to the stall and repeat the process of cornering the foal and raising his tail. If this is done, and the colt is pushed forward until pressure on the halter is relaxed, the handler should scratch his neck, then gently unsnap the lead shank while it is slack. The tail may then be released, and everyone should leave the stall.

Since most mares and foals are pastured, we want to issue a warning about turning them out with their halters on. Halters can get hooked on posts, and foals can get their legs tangled in their dam's halters while grazing. Veterinarians have noted that tragic accidents are caused by halters being left on in the pasture.

LEADING

When the young foal's dam is gentle, the work of early leading is simple. Attach a leadline to the halter of the foal, have a helper lead the mare, and walk around the stall. The foal will naturally follow at the side of his mother. From the stall you can proceed into a small lot or open field, letting the foal frisk along by his mother's side, using only leadline pressure to hold him back or steer him by the dam's left side.

The foal led at his mother's side may be stopped, petted, and gradually moved away from the mother, all with little fuss. His natural instinct to follow his mother gradually combines with the realization that the lead takes him where he should go, and soon the leader can take the foal farther and farther from the dam. The foal looks upon the handler as a friend and is inclined to go along with him without trouble. If the foal needs some encouragement to move forward, the handler may use the haunch-rope method. This foal is then said to be "pet-broken."

In the very early stages of the foal's life, one can teach him to lead by taking hold of the tail at the root, raising it with the right hand while the left hand grasps the halter to encourage the foal to step forward. Because some foals are stronger, older, and less co-operative, many people use the aid of a cotton haunch rope.

The rope should be 18 to 20 feet long. Make a loop at one end; then take about one-third the length of the rope and loop it over the hips and around the rear end of the colt. Run the remaining end of the rope through the end loop across the withers and forward through the halter. When attempting to lead the foal forward with the regular leadline, one can apply whatever pressure is necessary on the rear quarters with the haunch rope to get the colt to move forward (fig. 1A & B).

An older foal may be started in the same manner, but being older he may already be more independent of both mother and people and may therefore put up considerable resistance. A four- to five-hundred-pound foal can tax the strength of the stoutest man in a man-to-colt battle. Rather than fight it out (and perhaps have the foal win), it is wiser to use another method of control, called "force-breaking."

Despite the name, this is a humane yet effective method that

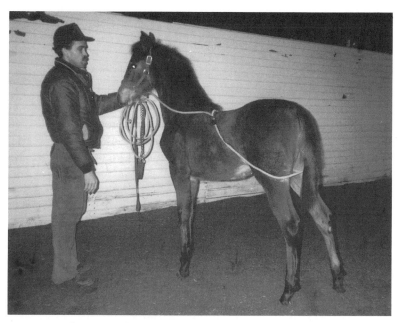

1A. Haunch-rope method may be used to encourage forward movement.

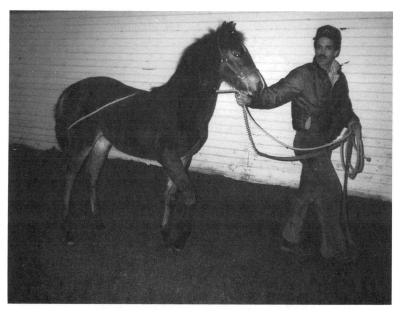

1B. Handler pulls the haunch-rope along with the normal lead shank.

9

has been used by farmers for years. All that is required is a heavy clothesline, or similar rope, about 15 feet long. A loop formed in one end is laid over the colt's loins and allowed to dangle about a foot below and behind the belly. The free end is then slipped through the loop and passed forward between the colt's front legs and up through the ring of the halter, to which the lead shank is attached. The handler now has the lead shank plus the rope line. As he pulls on the lead shank, he should follow with a pull on the rope line. The pressure from a new area may cause the colt to give a quick jump forward, releasing the pressure on the lead shank, which is what the handler wants. Before the handler again puts pressure on the lead line or rope shank, the colt should be allowed to stand for a while. Each time he responds to the "pulley" by a jump or step forward, he should be rewarded by released pressure on the lead shank. This process has an advantage over battling the halter alone, as pressure is exerted in a new area of the colt's body and less pressure need be placed on the halter itself.

To complete the process of force-breaking, you must also teach the colt to submit to being tied up. For this lesson it is best to use a stout post in the middle of a field, but a tree in the yard or a ring in the corner of a stall may be used instead. Lead the colt as close as possible to the post, and wrap the lead shank around it. Try to force the colt up to the post. If this method fails, use the rope pulley, with the lead shank and rope lapped around the post to keep the colt moved up to it. With young, tractable colts, this procedure is very simple, since one pull back tightens the rope and ends all resistance. With the older, more difficult colt, there may be some flips before he realizes that he must move forward to obtain relief from the pressure. Some colts will buckle their knees and lie down to resist being tied. They must be made to get up so that they can discover that forward motion will relieve the pull. One person alone may apply this method, but a helper who can urge the colt forward at times, and so strengthen the association in his mind between forward movement and relief, will hasten the process and make it much easier on the colt (fig. 2A & B).

Many colts have been trained to lead and be tied by using the kinder, slower process of petting and talking them into obedience. This works very well for the amateur who has a colt with a coopera-tive disposition, but it has drawbacks when applied to a more willful

2A.   Yearling is shown pulling against force-breaking rope.

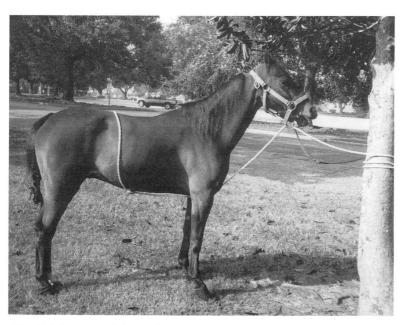

2B.   Colt has stepped forward in submission. He now knows that he must move forward to relieve the pressure.

11

animal or an older colt or horse. The colt that has been "force-broke" to tie and to lead rarely gives any trouble when being loaded into any kind of vehicle or led into any type of structure. He learned at an early age that there is just one solution to pressure on his halter to move, and that is to comply and move forward. The situation is similar to that of children who have learned to obey their parents at an early age. Disciplinary methods vary as greatly with horses as with children, but colts that learn to accept human authority early in life are more easily handled in all situations as mature horses. This does not imply unnecessary harshness or cruelty; it simply means using one's human head to stay a step ahead of the horse, demanding obedience to whatever is asked, and rewarding obedience immediately.

It is also useful to accustom the colt, at an early age, to cross-tying. It is usually not difficult to teach to a "force-broke" colt, but you may need some patience with others. Always cross-tie in the stall first. Be sure there is plenty of slack in the lines or chains. Do not leave the colt alone on the first few tries. In fact, do not leave any horse alone in cross-ties until you are confident that he is happy in the situation. Remember that many horses will cross-tie easily in their own stall but will become anxious and testy in an open area of a barn. When you are sure the colt is content in the cross-ties, you may shorten the lines to a reasonable control point. In case your horse gets into trouble you might also consider fastening the cross-ties to the horse's halter, using quick-release snaps; these are useful in the event of an accident when you need to release your horse quickly.

ADVANCED LEADING

After the foal has learned to walk with his mother, to walk with the handler alone, and to be tied up, he is ready for his graduate work in leading. (For the amateur owner of one colt, this even included a walk into the kitchen of the house!)

Before starting on advanced leading, you should handle the colt a great deal in the stall or paddock. Grooming is essential to good horse care, and it should begin with the young foal. However, do not start on a colt with a harsh currycomb or stiff brush. Instead, put a lead shank on the colt and brush his body with a soft brush; he will learn to enjoy the effect immensely. Begin with the shoulder and proceed to the back and chest, slowly working up to the neck.

Grooming the colt is a gradual process. From the body, move gradually to the forelegs, the rump, the belly, and finally down the legs. Deal with the head very carefully, for a colt that becomes head-shy at an early age will be increasingly troublesome as he grows older. At first, use only a rag or towel (but not a large, floppy one) on the head. Move slowly and easily about the head, rubbing in the direction of the hair and making little fuss over the ears until the colt thoroughly enjoys the grooming process. Good grooming accomplishes considerably more than keeping the colt clean, for it accustoms him to being handled all over, to movement all around him, to being pushed over to the right or left, and even to being asked to take a step backward occasionally.

This is also the time to include handling the legs and feet. Good grooming includes picking out the hooves. However, before you can do that you must accustom the colt to having his feet picked up. Facing the rear, take hold behind his ankle, bend his knee, and lift his foot up. In the first attempts, do not hold the foot up long; be content to get brief cooperation at each of the four legs. Pat the colt and speak nicely to him when he complies. Gradually lengthen the time you hold the foot up and start picking out the hoof (fig. 3). Of course, some people just leave it to the farrier to do this job at first, but you will gain his friendship by doing these preliminaries yourself!

Once the colt has become thoroughly accustomed to handling and simple leading, he is ready for more advanced work. For this the handler will need a leather lead shank, 6 or 8 feet long, and some sort of whip or stick. (A 3- to 4-foot sapling cut from willow or some straight, supple wood will do nicely.) Its purpose is not to hurt the colt but to act as an extension of the handler's arm in training exercises. A paddock or ring is desirable, though not essential, as the training area for advanced work. If a ring is available, however, use it, as the fence can afford a considerable advantage in control if a colt should become frightened or run away.

The first advanced exercise the colt is taught is to come immediately upon command. If the colt does not respond to a light touch on the halter, touch his rump lightly with the whip. If he steps forward, speak encouragingly. If he doesn't move, another light pull on the halter and light touch with the whip is in order. The trainer should be on the left side of the horse, in a position to pull forward on the halter with his left hand, while at the same time holding the whip in

13

3. When picking out the hoof, start at heel and work toward toe.

the right hand, ready to urge the colt forward. From this position the handler may also restrain the colt from moving too far ahead.

If properly schooled from the beginning, a colt will learn to lead nicely with no restraint from the lead line, walking straight ahead and just far enough to the side to avoid stepping on the heels of the handler. While the tiny foal may alternately be dragged forward or drag the handler, the colt must learn to lead pleasantly, walking with the handler. Nothing is more disagreeable than a horse that always pulls at his lead shank, and a horse that dawdles behind is almost as annoying. Therefore, it is very important to teach a colt to lead properly.

Once the colt has learned to come to a slight pull on his halter, with or without a tap of the whip, he is ready to learn to lead correctly. Hold the lead shank in your right hand with the excess length looped over to the left hand. The whip is held in the left hand. Thus, the right hand is in a position to raise or lower the colt's head, to encourage him to move forward or to hold him back if he tries to advance too quickly. The left hand holding the extra shank enables the handler to have two hands on the line in case of emergency, as when the colt jumps or bolts in fright. The whip in the left hand may be moved behind your back to tap the colt if he lags behind. The colt's shoulder should be just behind you, his head at your right hand. Do not allow him to bend his head away from you and push his shoulder into you. This will lead to eventual loss of control, especially after he has gained in age and strength. You should not allow him to turn his head toward you, either, or to nip at you or the lead shank. This is another bad habit that worsens with age.

Once the colt walks and leads nicely from the left side, teach him to lead from the right side. This is something that few owners, handlers, or trainers bother to do, but a really well-trained horse handles as easily from the right side as the left. If he has already been groomed a good deal he is used to having a person on either side, and learning to lead is merely a matter of reversing the earlier process. Perhaps one day should be spent coming up to the colt on the right side and accustoming him to moving forward in response to halter and whip used on the right. The colt that learns to handle and lead easily from either side will usually walk straight and will develop neither the "head-away, shoulder-to" habit nor that of turning his head toward the handler and swinging his hindquarters out.

After this phase of leading has been learned thoroughly and correctly at a walk, the colt is ready to be led at a trot. Another person's help will make this much easier, for the assistant can follow behind the colt with the whip. Pull lightly on the halter, and jog forward yourself a few steps; if the colt does not follow immediately, the assistant may tap him lightly on the quarters with the whip. If no assistant is on hand, reach behind your back with the whip that was used at a walk. Most colts are naturally eager to be off and going, so the trot is not hard to teach. However, holding him to a trot instead of a canter can be a challenge! An assistant behind sometimes causes the colt to canter off immediately, away from the whip. In this case, you and your assistant should attempt to coordinate your movements, or you should take the whip yourself. Alone, you can keep the colt under control from the front, allowing him to jog off only as much as desired, using the whip just enough to increase the pace if necessary.

15

STOPPING

It is very important to teach a colt to stop easily from any gait and to stand squarely when stopped. The colt's conformation will determine the best way for him to stand, along with his breed requirements. But whatever the breed, he should stand with his hind feet so positioned that legs and quarters appear perfectly straight and square from behind.

When teaching the colt to stand, work from the near (left) side and always position the hind legs first. Hold the halter firmly with the left hand, and either with the whip or with your hand on the colt's shoulder, push him back or pull him forward until the hind legs are even. Once the hind legs are positioned, concentrate on the forelegs. Do not kick at the fetlocks to move his feet forward; it is better to pull his head forward and toward the left, tapping the right foreleg on the forearm above the back of the knee. When he moves the right foreleg forward, repeat the procedure with the left, until the front legs are even and squarely under the colt. Avoid over-stretching. This is not necessary, does not show a colt to his best advantage, and can be a very hard habit to break once you have taught it. It takes much time and patience to attain a good stance, but if the colt is trained while young, a good stance on the lead will become a lifetime habit.

As soon as the colt stands squarely, reward him with kind words and a pat on the neck. It is enough to try to attain a square, quiet stance during the first few lessons. Later, when the colt has become accustomed to standing properly, you can concentrate on placing his head in just the right position by raising the chin or flexing the neck with halter pressure. Eventually, you should be able to stand in front of the posed colt, and get his ears pricked forward with a snap of the whip or by shaking an interesting object to draw his attention. However, a colt must be well schooled in standing still and square before you attempt to alert him into a showy pose.

LONGEING

Once the colt has been taught to lead and stand and is at least a year old, you can begin to teach him the rudiments of longeing. You will need a 20- to 30-foot longe line, for this will permit a large enough circle to avoid undue strain on immature legs and body. You will also need a light whip to encourage forward motion, and, if possible, a paddock or ring in which to begin the lessons.

Most trainers start longeing the colt to the left, this being the natural direction for a horse held on the left side. If the colt has already learned to lead perfectly, longeing should be relatively simple.

Start by leading the colt in a large circle, then gradually move away from him, making sure that he keeps moving forward as you back away. When the colt is about ten feet away from the handler and is still moving forward, you can use the whip to encourage him from behind. In longeing it is important for you to stay even with the colt's shoulder or slightly farther back. As soon as the colt shows a tendency to stop or turn, you can then immediately get behind the colt and drive him forward.

Just as it is important to handle and lead the colt from both sides, it is essential to teach him to longe in both directions. If he leads readily from the right side it will be no problem to follow the same procedure in teaching him to longe from the right, and he should always work equally well in both directions.

Too much longeing can be bad for a colt, and working on too small a circle can put an undue strain on his legs. (Wearing protective boots such as bell boots and splint boots may help your colt avoid some leg strain). The size of the circle should increase in proportion to your colt's size. Moderate amounts (ten or fifteen minutes of walking and trotting) of longeing are important preparation for later training routines and also afford adequate winter exercise where no paddock or ring is available.

The colt that has learned the lessons of leading, standing, coming, and longeing prior to the winter of his first year should be allowed to enjoy a vacation, to run and play for exercise, with only occasional training reviews. Overtraining of the colt, working him day after day on these routines, tends to produce a sour, bored animal that will be no pleasure to own and show in later years. In fact, there are many similarities between colts and human children of a comparable age. Once a lesson has been learned, you needn't overdo it, and you should let the colt relax and play between schooling sessions. When you do handle him, however, demand and expect the obedience that will be necessary to make him a pleasurable horse later.

CHAPTER 2

THE OLDER COLT

How some amateur trainers avoid getting killed will always be a mystery; surely much of their good fortune must stem from the horse's innate willingness to cooperate and to accept discipline. Horses are not very different from dogs, or even children, as far as discipline and affection are concerned—they need both, and a judicious blend makes life much more pleasant for all concerned. So let's assume that your colt has had both, and by now is halter-broken, leads nicely, stands tied quietly for grooming, and is well-mannered in the stall and out. At this point you are ready to start his real education and usefulness to you.

BITTING

The next step for any youngster past a year and a half of age, whether you intend him eventually for saddle or harness work, is bitting. These first bitting lessons may last for several weeks or even months, depending on the individual. (In fact, some horses will need occasional refresher courses in bitting throughout their lives.) The easiest way to introduce bitting is simply to snap a bit into the yearling's halter. Various special "yearling bits" are made for this purpose, but we prefer a regular jointed snaffle with a medium ring. The bit, which is snapped permanently to the off side of the halter, is eased into the colt's mouth gently and then snapped to the near side of the halter. Care should be taken to see that it is adjusted high enough to fit firmly, but not tightly, in the corners of the colt's mouth. Be sure that it is high enough not to dangle against the front teeth where the colt could loll his tongue up and over it.

At first the bit should be placed in the colt's mouth only for short periods of ten minutes or less, but gradually the periods can be lengthened up to a half hour. The colt should be left loose in his stall to experiment with the new gadget in his mouth. If after several days he persists in putting his tongue over the bit, rather than under it where it belongs, the bit probably needs to be raised in his mouth.

After the bit, the next step is the use of an actual bridle. By "bridle" we mean only the headstall and bit without reins; this may be a bitting bridle, a harness bridle, or a simple riding bridle from which the reins have been removed. While the plain snaffle with rings can be used if nothing else is available, there is a considerable choice of types if you are going to buy a bit specially for this purpose.

Closest to the plain ring snaffle is the egg-butt style. This can be a very nice bit for a colt, but it is usually difficult to find one in a small enough size to be suitable. The next alternative is the racing Dee bit, which comes in sizes small enough for the colt and also in varying weights of mouthpiece, so that one can usually get the size and weight desired. The Dee bit will not pull through the fractious horse's mouth as easily as will a ring-end bit, though the full-cheek bit is even more certain to stay balanced in the colt's mouth and not pull through. (On the other hand, the cheek ends can easily become entangled with other pieces of equipment, which makes it less convenient to use than the Dee bit.)

A last alternative is the half-cheek type of snaffle commonly found in driving harness bridles. As the cheek extends only below the bit, there is less trouble with entanglements with this bit than with the full-cheek. Our own preference of style is in this sequence: Dee bit, half-cheek, full-cheek, ring (fig. 4).

In addition to the style of bit, you must consider the size or width of the mouthpiece. The bit must be wide enough for the colt's mouth, yet should not hang limply, as when a five-inch bit is placed in a colt's mouth having only a four-inch width. Unless a colt's head is unusually big and coarse, a four-and-a-half-inch mouth is the most we need for breaking. While many colts require only a four-inch

19

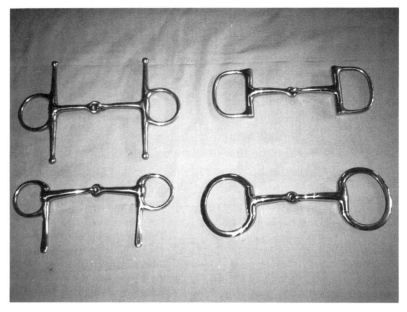

4. Snaffle bits. Clockwise from top left: full-cheek; Dee bit; egg-butt; half-cheek.

mouth, it is always better to have the bit slightly too wide across than to use a bit so small that it pinches the corners of the colt's mouth.

Finally, you must consider the thickness of the mouthpiece. For breaking colts the kind of bridoon snaffle bit normally used in a full bridle is too thin. The choice of thickness requires good judgment, for the bit must be thick enough to be mild to the colt's mouth and jaw, yet thin enough to fit neatly into the mouth without forcing open the jaws and causing discomfort. Here, again, a racing Dee bit usually can be found in the right weight as well as the proper width for almost any mouth.

BRIDLING

"Easy does it" is always a good rule when working about any young horse, and it is never more important than when commencing new lessons in the colt's education. It is important to move slowly and quietly, and speak softly and gently except when firmness or discipline are necessary.

The act of bridling the colt for the first time should be carefully thought out in advance, and the colt should be comfortable with your handling his head first. However, if the colt has been groomed regularly and has had his face brushed, his mane picked and brushed, and his ears fondled, he should not be head shy and it should be possible to bridle him the first time with little difficulty.

The bridle should fit properly, with the bit placed snugly but not harshly in the corners of the mouth. It is better to have the bridle a bit too big before putting it on; it is always easy to shorten the cheek straps after the colt is bridled, but too short a bridle will often result in a battle and a bad experience for the colt.

Approach the colt quietly, holding the bridle close to you and not allowing anything to jangle or flap to startle him. As you approach the colt's left side, slowly move the bridle forward and upward. The crownpiece should be held in your right hand and the bit in the left. By grasping the bit from the front with only your fingertips, you will have control of it, but your thumb will be free. Slowly raise the crownpiece upward until the bit is directly below the colt's mouth. If he does not open his mouth for it, gently insert the thumb of your left hand into the upper left corner of his mouth. As he opens his mouth in response to the thumb pressure, slip the bit up into his mouth with your fingers (fig. 5).

When the bit is in the colt's mouth, be careful not to pull the bridle up into his mouth too quickly. This is a time for utmost care. Holding the crownpiece steady, move it slowly upward, and pass it first over one ear and then the other. Most horsemen prefer to put the crownpiece over the right ear first, then work it onto the near side. However, if circumstances suggest that it would be easier to get the crownpiece over the near ear first, that is perfectly all right. The main precaution here is not to frighten the colt with any quick moves, not to jam the bit sharply up into his mouth, and not to hurt his ears in this first bridling attempt. Use extreme caution in each movement, for anything that upsets the colt now may stay with him for days or weeks to come.

Removing the bridle must be done just as carefully as putting it

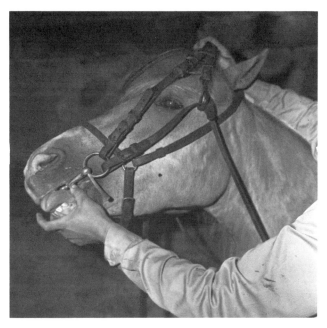

5. Left thumb opens colt's mouth and eases bit into it and over tongue as the right hand moves crownpiece over one ear.

on, and here again, extreme caution must be used to insure that nothing upsets the colt. A quick movement in taking the crownpiece off the colt's head may startle him into jumping back, pulling the bridle out of your hands. The loose bridle itself will become a source of fright. Another danger, even in routine unbridling, lies in pulling the bit too quickly from the horse's mouth. Support the crownpiece and wait until the colt himself opens his mouth (or you have reminded him to do so by using your left thumb); then slowly lower the bridle. Dropping the crownpiece too rapidly may result in the bit being caught in the colt's teeth, a situation that may make him rear or lunge to get rid of the jangling metal.

BITTING HARNESS

While the colt is learning to wear a bridle, he may as well become accustomed to other pieces of equipment also. If he has never worn

22

a sheet or blanket, it is a good idea to let him wear one so he becomes used to the feel of something resting on him and lightly encircling him. The sheet or blanket should be laid over the colt carefully and slowly (not thrown on) and the surcingles allowed to drop down slowly. Then you should reach slowly under the colt for the surcingles, fastening them so that they are loose but not dangling.

The proper time to start using a bitting harness depends upon the colt's temperament, his growth and development, and the purpose for which he is intended. The late fall and winter of the yearling year finds most colts that are destined for racing or shows already wearing a bitting harness. If the colt is to be used solely for pleasure and the owner is in no particular hurry, he may prefer to let the colt gain more growth. Some breeds mature more slowly than others, but in general, by the spring of the two-year-old year any colt should have grown enough to be ready for the bitting harness. (A few breeders prefer to let their horses run out and grow until they are late two-year-olds, bringing them up that fall for first lessons, but most amateur owners of just one or two colts would be wise to play with them earlier.)

A standard bitting harness made especially for the job is best. These are available both in all leather and in web, the latter being less expensive and just as satisfactory for the amateur owner (fig. 6A). However, it is possible to devise several substitutes. If you have some light driving harness, you may use the saddle and crupper pieces to rig up a homemade bitting harness. The shaft lugs, or tugs, should be tied down to the girth and then may be used in place of the lower rings on the bitting harness. If you have only a riding saddle to work with, even this will do as a substitute. The stirrups should be removed and the side reins attached to the billet straps beneath the saddle skirt. Another possibility is a regular surcingle. Get a saddler to attach three rings to it, one on each side about eighteen inches down from the top, and one right at the top center.

One warning before you start with the bitting harness: be sure not to pull everything up tightly on the colt at first. If a regular bitting harness is used, do not cinch it up too tightly or have the crupper pull up under the tail. If a saddle is used, it will need to be girthed up a bit tighter than a regular bitting harness or surcingle to prevent rolling. Even so, care must be taken to draw up the girth slowly and easily. When a girth is drawn up too tightly or quickly the horse may feel

23

"cinch bound" and react in a negative way, as by rearing or throwing itself. This may be true of older horses as well as young colts.

If one does not have a regular bitting harness with bridle, a regular snaffle bridle may be used. In this case the side reins running back to the surcingle must be improvised. Anything that simulates side reins may be used, even two lengths of clothesline with snaps at one end. (This works quite well if you snap one end to the bit first, then adjust the free end to the surcingle and tie it at the desired length.)

The first time side reins are used, they should be adjusted loosely enough to allow the colt considerable freedom. They should be kept loose for several lessons and then gradually shortened until they put pressure on the mouth and exert restraint through bit pressure. Tightening the side reins too quickly, or too snugly, may cause a colt to rear and throw himself, risking injury as well as inducing fear of the bitting harness (fig. 6B).

In succeeding lessons, as the side reins are shortened, you may help the colt learn to submit to the pressure by placing a hand on the bridge of his nose and pushing back, so that the pressure on his mouth is completely eased as he flexes his neck. The side reins should be shortened to the point where the head can flex naturally and easily, but only in the direction of rein pressure (fig. 6C).

6A. Colt is allowed to wear bitting harness with side and check reins very loose the first few times.

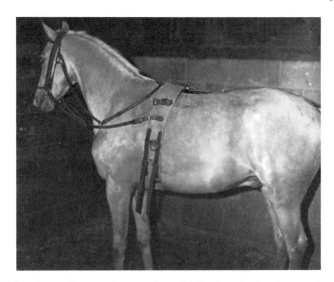

6B. Side-rein tensions are increased gradually, but check rein remains quite loose.

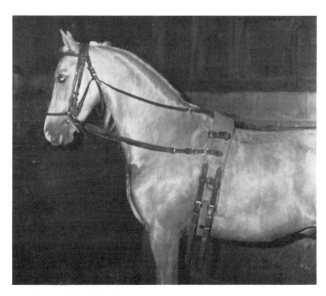

6C. Colt eventually learns to wear bitting harness with side reins adjusted for flexion and check rein shortened for head positioning as desired. Note that this colt is not resting on the bit.

We have not thus far discussed the special problems of putting the crupper under the colt's tail because the crupper is an optional piece of equipment for the owner who does not intend to break a colt to harness. However, for those who wish to prepare a colt for future driving, or whose bitting harness includes a crupper, preparation should be made to accustom the colt to it before any work with the bitting harness is started.

This preparation begins during the daily grooming of the colt by raising the tail slightly in brushing the hair, cautiously at first until the colt becomes accustomed to having his tail handled and moved by humans. Some horses have very flexible tails. Other tails are extremely stiff and unyielding, and colts with this type of tail are usually more sensitive to a crupper. To ease the insertion of the tail through the crupper loop, you may wrap the excess tail hair about the dock or base of the tail and hold it there in the right hand from the underside, while the crupper is put over the tail.

It is advisable to have someone help the first time you use the crupper, especially if the colt clamps his tail down or is too "handy with his heels" behind. The assistant may hold the colt's head and also steady the surcingle, allowing it to rest about halfway back between withers and loins to allow the crupper enough length to be put on easily. Then, raise the colt's tail with a firm grasp from the underside of the dock with your right hand while easing the crupper down over the upraised tail with your left hand. Ease the crupper forward and up under the tail to lie gently under the tail and against the body of the colt. Then place the surcingle in its proper position behind the withers and draw up the girth slowly. Let the tail down slowly when the crupper is in place, and be sure all tail hair is out of the way from under and around the sides of the crupper (fig. 7).

BITTING ADJUSTMENTS AND PROBLEMS

Once the colt has begun to bend his neck and head and to work the bit lightly in his mouth in the side reins, the check rein may be added. Those people training sport horses may choose to omit the check in their training procedures. The ordinary bitting harness bridle comes equipped with a side-check rein, which runs from the bit up through gag-runners fastened to the sides of the bridle below the ears. This style of check is most commonly used for early

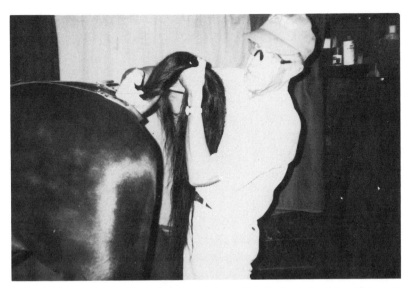

7. After crupper is in place, be sure to clear all hair from the sides of the tail.

bitting. The check rein should be fastened very loosely at first. Then, as with the side reins, it may be taken up gradually in succeeding lessons until the colt's head is in the desired position.

It is bad policy to keep the colt checked up too long, for if it becomes too tiresome for him, he may eventually learn to lean against the bit. Neither the side reins nor the check rein should ever be shortened so much that the horse cannot flex easily to them. Any further tightening may produce an unnatural, forced carriage for a short period but will not accomplish any real good for further riding and driving later.

Once the colt has become accustomed to wearing the bitting harness and to flexing nicely to it, he will benefit greatly from being exercised at the trot in the bitting harness. It is best to start with the reins loose and to shorten them gradually as the colt trots about and flexes to them. A paddock in which the colt can be turned out is ideal for letting him exercise himself at liberty in the bitting harness, learning to trot out, flex, stop, and respond to the pressures of the bit by his own will alone. At first some colts will kick hard and high at the crupper binding (fig. 8). It is wise to be sure that the crupper is not too tight, as noted above, but even so, during free

8. Don't be surprised if colt kicks when first turned loose in the bitting harness!

exercise the colt may try to buck, pulling the surcingle forward and the crupper tighter under his tail. However, most will give up the kicking when they find that it produces no relief from the crupper.

Useful as the bitting harness is, it can be dangerous if not used properly. The greatest dangers lie in opposite extremes: putting the rigging on the colt with everything adjusted too long and loose; or setting the side reins and check rein too short. Both extremes are like the notion that if one pill is good, two would be better.

In fact, however, either extreme will produce a horse that is heavy on the bit and lugs or leans on the reins against the rider's hands. The aim of bitting is to produce a horse that is light on the bit and responsive and that will flex his jaw and neck to proper pressures. Too much, too long, or too tight a use of the bitting harness will produce the opposite results.

When an older horse has already acquired these undesirable traits and needs rebitting, one should also go back to the bitting harness. In such cases, a twisted wire bit may be needed in place of the smooth snaffle in order to reawaken the sensibilities of his hardened mouth and make him responsive again. In other respects this sort of horse should be started out in the same manner as a colt, with loose side reins and checking, and only gradually brought up to the desired position and responsiveness. Short periods of bitting work (ten to fifteen minutes, never more than thirty minutes) are the order. Never let either the colt or the older horse stay in the bitting harness so long or so tightly that he learns to merely lean his head and neck on the bit.

TRAINING IN THE BITTING HARNESS

By the time the colt is ending his yearling year or starting his two-year-old year, he is ready to prepare for real work. Longeing the colt in the bitting harness is the first step toward the full control you need before driving him in a cart. Make sure the side reins are taut enough to keep the colt's head facing straight but not so tight that he is restrained in any way from moving forward. The best way to hook up the longe is to buckle on a leather chin strap with a ring between the two rings of the snaffle. The longe line should be attached to this extra ring, affording control through the bit, but not exerting continuous side pressure. Of course, if the horse is easily handled, the longe line can simply be snapped into the snaffle ring on the side nearest the handler. (In this case, the line must be changed to the other ring when the direction is reversed.) However, if the colt or horse is larger or has indicated that he is hard to hold, it is safer to use a longe with a chain shank, and run the chain through the snaffle ring on the near side, under the chin, and snap it to the bit ring on the far side. If you do not feel that your colt requires this measure, and you prefer a ring under the chin, the halter may be left on under the bridle and the longe snapped to the halter ring. As the horse is already controlled to some extent by the bitting harness, the nose pressure of the halter will provide enough additional control.

The final choice of longeing method will depend upon the individual horse. One that becomes perfectly broken to longe will eventually go around at the end of the line without pulling, whatever length is given him, and be perfectly responsive to commands to walk, trot, canter, stop, or even reverse.

For all proper longeing work, a whip is essential. If the horse is to circle counter-clockwise, the handler stands even with the horse's shoulder (never in front of him) and holds the longeing rein in his left hand, with the whip in his right hand extended somewhat toward the horse's rear. The animal is thus contained between the longeing rein in front and the whip behind. The whip is sometimes omitted for exercising the colt that has learned his first longeing lessons well, but it is an essential aid in teaching any horse to really march forward, flexing his hocks well up under him and flexing his head and neck to the bitting harness. Proper training in longeing will exercise the horse while developing correct form at his gaits, and will teach him responsiveness to bit pressures. The colt will also learn to bend his body on the circle while keeping his head straight. (When longed without the bitting harness, horses are inclined to move around the circle with their heads turned in and quarters turned out.) The goal is to have the horse track straight while properly bending around turns.

In the bitting harness a colt may also be taught a great deal about collection at all gaits; you may restrict his speed and the diameter of his circle by shortening the longe line, but still maintain propulsion from his quarters with the whip. A horse that is longed must learn to balance himself and thus will gain suppleness and surefootedness—most desirable qualities in a horse for any purpose.

Once the colt is familiar with longeing procedures, you may do actual training work with him when he is turned loose in a small paddock while wearing a bitting rig. You can compel the colt to exercise himself in a controlled manner by getting him to move at liberty around the perimeter of the fence. Your voice and use of the whip (if the colt has had previous longe-line work) will act in place of the line, while more freedom and space will teach him further looseness and relaxation in the harness and perhaps develop a faster, freer trot than can be attained on the small circle of the longe line.

Working a horse in a bitting harness is the best exercise for the horse with an amateur trainer, for here the horse is training himself to be responsive.

DRIVING IN LONG LINES

Once the colt has become responsive to the bitting harness and to longeing, he is ready for further education. Driving in long lines is the next step in his education. Almost any style of line may be used as long reins, but we prefer web line, or a clothesline type of cotton, or soft nylon rope, about one-half inch in diameter. These lines should be between fifteen and eighteen feet long. The length depends to some extent upon the size and conformation of the colt and the personal preferences and abilities of the handler. Lines that are too long are awkward and may become entangled, whereas lines too short are dangerous, placing the driver close enough to the colt to be kicked.

Always longe the colt lightly in the bitting harness before attempting to drive him in long lines. He weighs a great deal more than a person, after all, and is quite capable of departing, with or without driver, should it enter his head to do so. However, it is not necessary to exercise the colt to the point of exhaustion or boredom, just to the degree that his attention does not give way to exuberance.

The long lines are run through the lower rings of the bitting harness (or through the shaft loops on a driving harness) and attached to the bit. Usually it is best to attach the long line on the near side first, so that you can turn the colt toward you if he should jump. Then lay the other line gently over his back, move around in front of him, pull the snap end through the lower ring of the surcingle, and then attach it to the bridle ring. Now move back to the left side of the colt, and gather up the lines.

It is helpful to have an assistant for the first driving lesson. He should hold the colt lightly by the head while the driver slowly eases the right line down over the colt's right hindquarter and places himself behind the colt. The assistant then leads the colt off for the first few steps, after which the driver should be able to handle the animal. The colt can be expected to flinch a bit from the feel of the lines about his quarters, but unless he really tries to run or lunge off the ground, the driver should just ease him along forward rather than pulling him sharply to stop. Many colts learn to be balky by being stopped for every wrong move in their first lessons. If the driver can herd him about under some control during the initial few lessons, it

31

is better to let the colt keep going forward and to avoid jabs on his mouth.

If the colt is wearing the bitting harness with side and check reins lightly fastened, he is already under some control. The driver has him between two lines and can effectively steer him in most directions, though not in tight circles. By having the lines run through the lower ring of the bitting harness, the driver can usually prevent the colt from whirling in an attempt to see what is behind him, for the low line affords control over the hind end as well as the front (fig. 9). When lines are run up high, as through the terrets of a driving harness, the colt can swing his quarters under the lines and then is almost impossible to guide the first few times.

The first lessons in ground driving should be given at a walk or jog. Gradually the driver may ask for a trot, for as long as the driver can run, and then ask for stops. When the colt is driving nicely, the stops may be extended into formal "parking," feet placed squarely and the colt set up alertly. Finally, the colt should be taught to back up. The first attempts at backing should stop with the first step or two rather than several steps. When the driver pulls, he should then release the pressure immediately when the colt yields the first backward step.

As the driving lessons progress on the ground, the handler should dispense with the side reins and check rein, and use just the ordinary bit with long lines attached. To be sure the colt is perfectly supple and responsive, he may be driven in circles, similar to longeing, with the driver still in a driving position having eased himself towards the center of the circle (fig. 10). A final exercise in responsiveness may be to dispense with the lines through the side rings, merely attaching them to the bit. If the driver can then drive the colt anywhere without his turning about or ducking; if he can circle him, guiding from the near rein directly and the off rein over his neck; if he can turn him about easily even with the rein across his neck—then the colt is truly responsive to the bit and ready to be hitched or ridden.

LIMITATIONS OF BITTING

A point to remember in connection with bitting is that the horse's conformation limits the accomplishments of any type of training. Despite all the treatises on straight legs, short backs, sloping shoul-

9. *Driving in long lines is done here with side reins and check attached. Note that long lines run through lower rings of surcingle.*

10. *Once colt has learned absolute responsiveness to the bit, stopping and turning, he may be circled in long lines alone.*

33

ders, neat heads, etc., some individuals have almost all these desirable features but are simply not arranged in a package that lends itself to suppleness. On the other hand, there are colts whose conformation is anything but perfect, but which nevertheless are put together in a fashion that permits training and improvement.

From a training standpoint, many limitations are involved with the structure of the head and neck. A horse with generally poor conformation may well have a head that "hangs on his neck" just right, a head that can be set easily and lends itself to a good mouth, so bitting should be accomplished relatively easily. Another that seems to be a perfect model of conformation may have his head and neck joined in such a way that his throatlatch is thick. Such a horse tends to be inflexible and hardmouthed, although with careful and patient training he may be given a perfect carriage.

To describe a well-set head and neck for a horse headed for the show ring, we say that the neck itself should come out of the shoulder high at the top and deep at the bottom, with a long and graceful top line. The throatlatch should be fine and slender, and the neck should be long and supple enough to assume an elevated position easily. A horse with a short top line can never flex at the poll well enough to carry a high, well-set head, nor indeed can he carry it easily in any position required by his training, other than straight out and low.

The distribution of the horse's body weight also affects his adaptability to saddle and harness. Some horses just naturally look good in harness and are said to be harness types. Others do not look so good in harness, no matter how well they are trained. An elegant carriage of head and neck is a first essential for a stylish harness horse. Another essential is a smooth top line from the wither back, ending with a high-set tail, carried gaily. A horse that is high up on his legs and short in body and neck never looks suited to harness. Neither does a short, steep-rumped horse.

Aside from physical structure, there are also psychological limitations to the accomplishments of bitting for some horses. Like people, horses vary in character and tractability. While some horses require months of bitting-harness work before they are responsive enough to hitch, others quickly become dull and bored with the whole process. The details of approach and technique are not the same for every horse, and the trainer must be the judge. In the last analysis, judgment marks the difference between the best and the average,

34

even among professional trainers of long experience. Knowing when to let up on the horse and when to stop at a certain point of training can be the difference between success and failure.

A few points in the training procedure are sometimes considered controversial, or at least open to argument. First is the choice of side reins between those made of leather and those that are only part leather, with some sort of rubber or elastic shock-absorbers added. Many horsemen prefer the latter type on the theory that the colt can then play more with the pressure on the bit, and that the side reins can be shortened more quickly over fewer training sessions with less danger of the colt throwing himself. Most professional horsemen, however, choose solid leather side reins on the theory that there should not be any give to the reins, that the horse must learn to respect the pressure and never find that he can push out against them. We have concluded over the years that this "ungiving" side-rein method is best. Our experience is this: with elastic side reins a colt is tempted to obtain relief from pressure by pulling against the reins and thus learns to try to take the bit away from the driver or rider. Solid leather reins make him submit to the pressure in order to obtain relief.

A second question is when to attach the check rein on those horses to be schooled with one. Many horsemen support the proposition that the check rein should be attached first, teaching the colt to go with his head up before side reins are applied. That this is common practice is obvious to any professional horseman who gets spoiled horses to remake, for among the most common "problem horses" are those which will not flex and travel with their heads set gracefully. The experienced horseman can detect this problem the first time he bridles the horse, for a horse that has been properly mouthed will drop his chin and flex his neck at the lightest touch on the reins from somebody on the ground, while the "problem horses" stick their noses into the air the minute the reins are touched. This is a common trait of the horse that has been broken to the check first and has also been checked too high thereafter.

When bitting the horse, especially for saddle work, teach the side-rein pressures first. It usually pays to work the youngster for some time with side reins only, until he has learned to flex to the pressure of the bit. A few will overflex by dropping their chins toward their chests, but even this is to be preferred to the horse who throws

35

11. Having learned to flex to side reins, horse now has head set and mouth closed.

his nose out and head back to a check rein. Our aim is to obtain an immediate response to bit pressures and to teach the colt that he must draw his head back until it is perpendicular to the ground and relax his jaw to the rein pressure to obtain relief. A colt that is wearing the side reins properly and lightly is said to be "barely touching the bit" (fig. 11).

Elevation of the head, if desired, is achieved through intelligent checking after the colt has submitted to the side reins. One starts with the check fairly loose and gradually shortens it until the horse's head is set at as good an angle as his conformation will allow. Some horses are able to set their heads so proudly that a perpendicular line can be drawn from the throatlatch along the underside of the neck to the chest. Other horses can never achieve this, even through training, by reason of their straighter shoulders and shorter necks. In any case, you must avoid leaving a colt checked too long, as he will then rest his head on the bit and check rein, encouraging future lugging on the bit and deadening the bars of the horse's mouth (fig. 12). The bitting process should continue only long enough to accomplish the colt's submission to bit pressure. Short lessons at first may be followed by longer ones, never lasting more than thirty minutes. Take care

12. With overcheck and side reins too tight, horse opens its mouth and leans on the bit.

that the colt does not become tired or bored, for like a child, he will become sulky and rebellious.

SUMMARY

Before proceeding from ground work to actual riding or driving, let us review the preparatory steps that assure readiness for further schooling.

First, the colt should accept the normal daily routine of cleaning his stall, feeding, and grooming with complete confidence in his handlers. An animal that still shows suspicion toward man in any of these routine chores is certainly not ready for advanced schooling, at least not in the hands of an amateur.

If the colt is shy in the stall when being worked around, or jumpy during grooming, or frightened by ordinary, normal noises, the owner should take warning that his colt either is not ready for further schooling or is one of those particularly nervous individuals that should be turned over to a capable professional for introduction to actual driving or riding.

When one is dealing with a nervous horse, quiet, firm know-

37

how is essential. The selection of the professional is highly important, as turning this colt over to the wrong person might be the worst
move an owner could make. In most cases an older horseman who
has proved himself a master of many types of horses, and whose
training methods are quiet and unhurried, should be preferred over
the more daring, dashing type of trainer. Mistakes made at this point
in training may be irreparable.

In addition to a pleasant stall disposition, the animal should lead
well; stand well when tied, either to a corner or crosstied; and be
responsive to words or signals to move forward, step, or back up.

Use of the voice in the schooling of a colt is much more important to the amateur than to the professional. Spoken words, as such,
mean little to a horse, but they can convey definite meanings when
repeated in the same way, with the same intonation, in similar situations. For example, the word "whoa" has universally come to mean
"stop," and for most purposes it should be a forceful command that
means "stop" and nothing else. However, it is used by many riders
and drivers to simply slow or quiet a horse down, and many show
riders are heard saying "whoa" or "whup" in a higher, quicker intonation while riding at speed, thereby using the term merely as an
encouragement to go but to remain at the chosen gait.

The pitch and volume convey meaning to the horse, and the
amateur should remember that voice commands can be very helpful
in training if used with consistency. A word used in praise can, by
tone, convey the meaning to the horse, and a sharp word can often
be more effective than physical punishment. One should never rely
on voice commands alone but reinforce them with their associated
signals, in all steps of training. The horse is a creature of pattern and
habit, and the trainer should consider this in training. A horse's response to pattern and habit can be used as a help in training, and bad
training habits will also be remembered—an excellent reason to avoid
repeating them.

For training, however, the voice may be used with excellent
results if the limitations are recognized. When you urge the colt forward, repeat "walk" in a quiet, steady voice. Order a "trot" in the
same way, with a little more insistence and volume. If one is training
a colt for harness work, the canter should be avoided, either on the
longe line or in driving lines. Therefore, teaching the voice command "canter" should be avoided unless one is preparing a three-

year-old horse for riding. Harness gaits are strictly the walk and the trot, and the canter should always be discouraged, regardless whether one is planning to drive for show or pleasure.

The colt is ready to be advanced to further harness and saddle work when he is relaxed and confident in the stall and while being led, groomed, or tied; is not upset by ordinary noises and occurrences; accepts the bridle and harness; and performs willingly in longeing harness and long lines. If there is any question in the owner's mind regarding these accomplishments, he should either spend more time in perfecting the preparatory steps or consider seeking professional help with the horse.

CHAPTER 3

BREAKING THE COLT
TO DRIVE

•————————

THE ADVANTAGES OF DRIVING

At this point, readers who are primarily interested in riding are probably ready to skip ahead to the next chapter, and indeed, most trainers proceed directly to riding if the colt is old enough to be ridden and is working well on the longe and in long lines. However, while this chapter is addressed more to driving enthusiasts than to riders, there is much to be said for the idea that all colts should get at least a brief education "between the shafts," and the rider who is willing to spend a little extra time sitting behind his horse rather than on top of him will surely be handsomely rewarded for his pains.

People who only know about riding may wonder why any effort should be expended in breaking a horse to drive. The basic answer is to develop both mouth and manners. If one has any doubts about the value of harness work in this regard, he should investigate some of the age-old texts on problem horses. The solutions are always given in terms of dominance acquired by man over the horse from the ground! The day of just putting a saddle and bridle on a wild horse and "riding him out" has long since passed. Even the most qualified of the "cowboys" now subscribe to a more orderly and scientific breaking process. Some people object to the use of the term "breaking," preferring the terms "training" or "making." Actually the training methods approved by the best horsemen for breaking a colt do not in any way "break" the spirit but are designed to instill respect for human direction and submission to the tools man uses.

At the age of two, most colts can physically stand pulling a light cart when they could hardly carry a man of average weight. Thus, driving gives owners a chance to educate and enjoy a colt at an age that does not permit carrying much weight. The driving should be done moderately at first, both in gait and in distance. At this time the colt has the opportunity to learn obedience to his handler and also to develop physically from extended periods (up to a half hour) of walking and trotting without the hindrance of weight on his back. Country driving for short periods can improve the walk and trot immensely if there is no undue pressure for speed or action. The important thing to remember is to keep the load light and the work moderate according to the terrain.

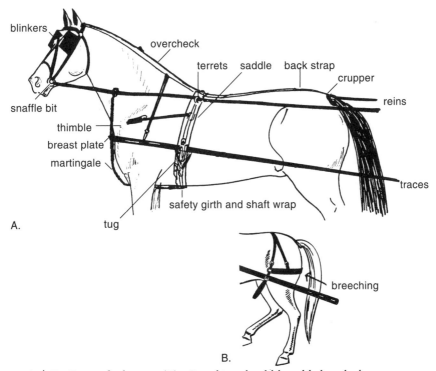

13A & B. Parts of a harness (A). Breeching should be added to the harness for country driving to hold cart back on hills (B).

As the colt grows and matures, his trotting strength can be improved greatly in harness. Here he will learn to balance himself without carrying a human weight. The owner may experiment with various shoes to find those which produce the best balance and action, or speed, desired for this horse's future. The owner may work toward perfecting his horse's mouth and manners, getting him to trot loosely in harness with style and animation while remaining perfectly responsive to the lightest touch on the bit. In short, whether driving is an end in itself or simply a means to an end, it is a wonderful way to develop the horse's physical and mental capabilities.

PRELIMINARIES

Several preliminary steps must be accomplished before you can actually put your colt to the shafts, even though he is already well drilled in the bitting harness and long lines. First you must ready the actual driving harness (fig. 13A & B), for no matter what kind of substitute you have used in training, the time has come when the harness must be "sound." This may mean a different bridle and harness than you used in preliminary training, and a colt that has done all his preliminary work in an open bridle (without blinders) or a side-check bridle will be understandably confused if he is suddenly placed in a driving-harness bridle with blinders and an overcheck that has an additional bit.

Whichever driving bridle you use, take pains to fit the actual driving harness to the colt very carefully. It may also be difficult for the amateur to ease a heavier harness onto a green colt. The approach and method of bridling is the same, but here you must be careful to keep both bits together between the fingers of your left hand and to ease both gently into the colt's mouth at the same time (fig. 14). Fitting the headstall over the ears should be done slowly and quietly. Care should be taken to see that the blinders do not jab the colt in the eyes. If the bridle is new or stiff you should work the leather before putting it on so that the blinders open outward rather than pulling in against the colt's eyes. A running martingale may also be added at this point. It should be adjusted so driving lines run in a straight line from the bit through the terrets. A shoestring tied to the martingale ring on one side can be laid up over the neck and tied to the ring on the other side to keep the martingale from slip-

14. Alternative method of bridling with overcheck bridle and blinders: Overcheck bit is held up with crownpiece in right hand while left hand inserts main snaffle bit only. The check bit is inserted after bridle has been put on colt.

ping down and catching on the bit. This is also the time to be certain the horse is not girthed too tightly and the check fits comfortably.

After the body of the harness and the bridle are in place, give the colt a quick refresher course on his earlier driving in long lines (fig. 15). If the bridle is new and the colt seems nervous, it is best to run the long lines through the shaft lugs rather than the terrets so that you closely duplicate his first driving in lines. Care must be taken in attaching the check rein if the colt is not used to the overcheck. Again, this should be attached loosely at first and then gradually shortened to the desired head carriage.

When you are satisfied that the colt is wearing the regular harness quietly and calmly and is driving nicely in the lines, take the next preparatory step before actually hitching to a cart. The breastplate with traces may now be added. You may add short pieces of rope to the ends of the traces, extending their length by at least six feet more. Then have an assistant hold the ends of the traces, via the

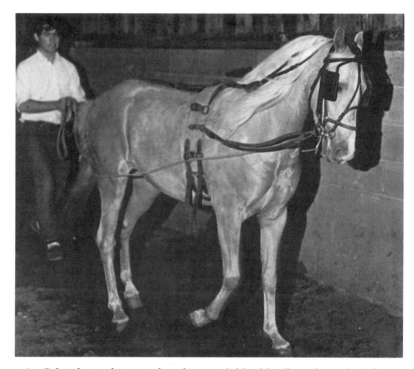

15. Colt is being driven in long lines with blind bridle and overcheck bit.

ropes, and gradually lean back on the traces as you drive the colt forward (fig. 16). This will get the colt accustomed to the feel of the weight on his chest and shoulders. Of course you may tie the extenders together and exert this same pressure yourself while driving, if you cannot find a helper. But it is best done with one person to drive and another to hold back on the traces.

If there is the least bit of uncertainty on the part of the horse in this process, be sure to work with him slowly and carefully, as too rapid progress may lead to a mismove that could cause damage to vehicle, horse, and handlers. A very quiet and sensible colt may learn the routine of bitting, long-lining, and hitching preparations in as little as one month. Others more spirited or suspicious may require closer to a year! The trainer must make the decision when to hitch, and it is a momentous one, for an error in starting too early may mean failure in ever having a suitable driving horse. When in doubt, always give the colt a little more time.

16. Driver and her assistant getting colt used to weight on his chest and shoulders by leaning back on traces.

Some people prefer to hitch a colt to "poles" a few times before actually hitching to a cart, but we believe, like most professional horsemen, that if the colt is ready to be hitched he might just as well be hitched to a good cart as to poles. Poles were a more desirable means of breaking heavy horses years ago, when much of the driving was aimed at pulling loads on the ground. Then it was advisable to have the horse used to poles and straps hitting low around his hind legs, or even hitting his heels. Very few horses today are required to pull anything other than a light cart or buggy, and an amateur can run into just as much trouble with poles as with a cart.

If you have access to training shafts we do recommend driving the colt with this apparatus in order to accustom him to the feel of shafts before actually hitching him (fig. 17A–C).

Before proceeding further you must now consider your choice of vehicle. There are all types of theories on breaking carts, some having special safety devices such as brakes and back extensions to

45

keep the cart from tipping over if a colt rears. Carts with these safety features are fine if they are not too heavy. However, if the job of breaking the colt to the bitting rig, harness, and long lines has been done fully and carefully, any good sound two-wheeled cart will do. Actually a sulky or light cart is often preferable to the heavy, so-

17A. Training shafts.

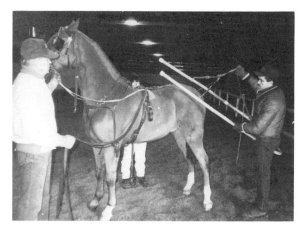

17B. Placing training shafts on colt. Note use of person on off side to help put shaft through tug.

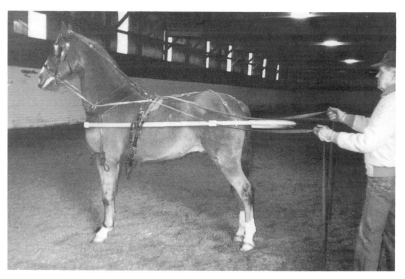

17C. Colt ready to move off.

called safety breaking carts, which scare a horse by their very bulk and weight or make him hesitant to pull the heavy load.

Remember, it is most important that the equipment—harness and cart—be strong and safe. Many more accidents occur because of bad equipment than because of bad manners on the part of the horse!

HITCHING TO THE CART

At last the great day arrives. You are sure the colt will respond nicely to your every command, voice, and bit. He trusts you and all the rigging you have put on him. This is the day you have decided to hitch the colt.

First, always be sure that the colt has had exercise and is not "fresh" when you get ready to hitch him the first time. Let him see the vehicle; walk him around it; drive him in the long lines with someone pulling the cart behind so he becomes accustomed to the sound behind him. Never attempt to hitch a colt alone the first few times.

Wherever possible, enlist two assistants for the first hitching, and remember that the skill and experience of your helpers will have a bearing upon your success. One good helper is better than two who don't know what they're doing. If you must use an inexperienced helper, get one who is calm, quiet, sensible, and strong.

The colt should wear a halter under the driving bridle. If he usually wears one in his stall, just leave it on and put the driving bridle on over the halter. Take a long rope (one of the long-line reins will do), run it through the ring of the snaffle on the near side up over the colt's head just behind the ears, and attach it to the right ring of the snaffle bit (fig. 18). A regular lead shank may be attached to the regular lead ring of the halter. This lead shank attached to the halter is the one to use. The rope should have no pressure on it. The rope over the horse's head is an emergency precaution, to be used only if absolutely necessary.

Having taken these precautions, next drive the colt around the cart, with an assistant holding the lead line at his head and also holding the longer emergency line. Stop the colt in front of the cart. Have the assistant stand at the colt's head, holding him lightly by the rings on each side of the bit, but with the lead rein and the emergency rope also in hand. As one assistant stands facing the colt, holding

47

18. For first hitching, long line is run through near ring of snaffle bit, over colt's head, and snapped to off-side snaffle ring to act as a safety line. Helper stands in front of colt with a light hold on each side of head.

him lightly and talking gently, bring the cart up to the colt quietly. If there is a second assistant, have him work from the off (right-hand) side of the horse to assist in running the shafts through the tugs. Unwind the traces and attach them. Last, adjust the safety girth, or tie-down (fig. 19). While the harness should fit well, it should not be so tight anywhere as to unduly bind the green colt. The check rein (either sidecheck or overcheck) should be fairly loose (fig. 20).

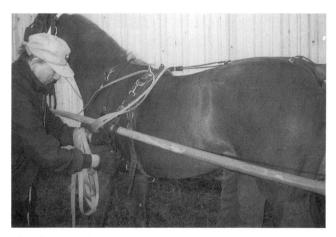

19. Colt is between shafts with traces fastened. Assistants are wrapping safety girth on shaft on near and off sides.

20. Driver has reins and safety line in hand as he attaches check rein.

Once the colt is hitched, let the assistant start leading him slowly while you walk alongside the cart, or preferably behind it (fig. 21). Having worked in traces previously, the colt should find pulling a light sulky no effort, but a heavy cart may bewilder him, and the driver may find it advisable to push the cart slightly to help at the start. If the colt lunges forward the assistant should try to stay with him, controlling him with the lead line and striving to keep him

21. Helper starts to lead colt off as driver walks beside cart.

49

22. Satisfied that colt has adjusted to the feel of the cart, driver gets in while helper remains near colt's head.

23. With driver in cart, helper starts colt into a trot. If driver is satisfied, helper may then release lead line. Note that driver retains safety line.

moving in a straight line. Too often the assistant tries to stand still and stop the colt suddenly, causing him to turn and tip the cart. Some colts will start off quite slowly and easily, but more will make their first moves in jumps, stops, and starts at the feel of the new equipment and the sound of the cart. It is best to have the colt in a large ring or an open field for this first hitching so that there will be plenty of room to work in and no sharp turns to make. The feel of the shafts touching the shoulders during turns is one of the most frightening things to colts, so turns should be made wide and gradually.

If all goes well, unhitch the colt after only five or ten minutes of driving at a walk or slow trot. (For unhitching and unharnessing, see pages 53-54.) If possible, hitch up the colt again the next day, following the same procedure. After walking behind the cart for a few minutes with the helper still holding the lead line and the emergency rope, gently get in the cart (fig. 22). If the colt shows no fear at this new weight, you may try jogging slowly, with the helper running alongside (fig. 23). He may then gradually ease back and away from the colt. If the colt is going along nicely, the helper may be able to gently detach the lead line, and let out the emergency rope until it is long enough to let him sit on the seat of the cart. The colt is being driven by the handler, but the helper still has the emergency line and can jump off and use it if necessary.

There is no rule for how many lessons it takes to have a colt "broke" to harness. Some colts will let the helper get in the cart on the second hitching. Sometimes the trainer can even take the emergency rope himself and drive without the assistant during the second lesson. But some colts will need to wait for several hitchings, and others will be calm and quiet during the first lesson or two and then suddenly try to lunge or run. Some will be ready for ordinary hitching after three lessons; others may take thirty. Some may always be nervous and jittery about being hitched and yet be perfectly fine horses to drive once they are under way. Hitching and driving regularly are necessary to make any colt a reliable driving horse. Ordinarily the check rein may be shortened as the colt becomes accustomed to driving. However, it usually is left loose until the horse is fully hitched and the driver is ready to go.

In the early driving of colts care must be taken not to force him to pull for more than fifteen minutes. He should not be asked to back during early driving lessons, as this may cause the habit of backing

51

too freely or of trying to run back at the sight of something strange. Likewise, one should not jab on the colt's mouth or try to stop him too abruptly in early lessons, lest he become stale and learn to balk. He cannot be expected to drive like an old horse without lots of practice, so don't expect to have a finished driving horse overnight. The best advice is always to "Make haste slowly" (fig. 24).

The reader will note that we have discussed hitching the colt with a light harness only and that no mention has been made of a kicking strap. If the colt has been brought along slowly and properly, no kicking strap should be needed in hitching, though many people would not think of hitching a colt the first few times without one. This is a matter of preference, but we have never found one necessary and find that many trainers do not use them.

However, if one is developing a colt for real country driving, up and down hills, a heavier harness with breeching is advisable (fig. 25). In this case it is wise to add the breeching during the last phase of bitting, longeing the colt with it until he is used to the movement about his quarters. He should also be long-lined with the full

24. Green colt being driven successfully and safely enough to take a passenger.

25. Vermont country outing. Grace M. Yaglou driving two Welsh mares in heavier carriage harness with full breeching. Jean Mack is passenger.

breeching added to the basic harness. Some people prefer to hitch the first few times without breeching and then accustom the colt to breeching later. If one wishes to hitch the first time with full breeching, a kicking strap might be advisable. Full breeching will most certainly be necessary for any driving up and down hills with a four-wheeled buggy, though not for driving on fairly level land. Some light harnesses come with "thimbles," which run from the harness saddle to the front point of the shafts, thus acting as a "stop" to forward movement of the buggy. Such thimbles, plus the wrapping of the safety strap, will control forward motion of the vehicle under normal driving conditions, but they will not do for long or steep downhill driving.

When you unhitch and unharness, the assistant should once more stand in front of the colt, holding him lightly on each side of the bit. Traces should be loosened and wound up, then the safety girth detached from the shafts (fig. 26A). A word of caution: a harness bridle should never be removed while the horse is still hitched to the cart! Finally, the cart should be pushed back so the shafts clear the legs, and the shafts then raised so that the cart can be pushed back without any danger of jabbing the colt in the sides (fig. 26B). The colt should then be walked quietly to the barn and the harness then removed piece by piece in a gently and orderly way (fig. 27A–C, & 28).

Until the colt is thoroughly settled in harness, driving should be confined to a two-wheeled cart. In a cart the colt can make quite a few little lunges, or even fairly short turns, without causing an upset. A buggy does not turn as easily or pull as lightly. It is best not to back the colt in harness until he performs smoothly at the walk, trot, and stop commands and backs very well in the long lines. Occasionally we encounter a horse that hates to back. In such cases it is best to drive him tight up into a corner in the lines, so that you can take advantage of his inability to go forward while pulling back on the lines and giving the "back" command. Any step or two back should be rewarded with praise; never insist upon prolonged backing. There is little need to back up in harness; on the contrary, backing up is to be avoided in most cases, as a horse running backward in harness can cause serious accidents. The finished driving horse should be willing to back several steps with good manners, but this is not something that you should strive for in early driving lessons.

Most problems in harness work are the result of too little preliminary work: lack of confidence in the handler on the part of the horse, improper equipment, or breakage of equipment. Any of these deficiencies can easily produce the "runaway," the "kicker," or "balker." If the amateur owner has any doubts in his mind about whether his colt is ready to hitch and drive to the cart, he should wait or seek professional help. If he encounters any real difficulties in the process of hitching, he should hasten to procure professional help before the problems become insurmountable.

The special requirements for various driving competitions will be discussed later. We will just mention here that overchecks and martingales are not allowed in some classes of competition. If your horse has been broken well, he should perform quite acceptably without check or martingale.

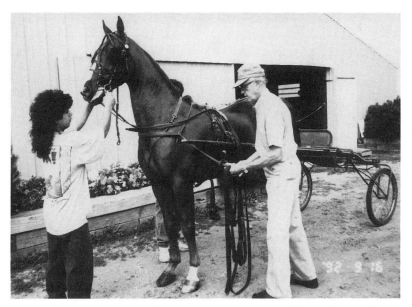

26A. Unharnessing colt. Safety girth has been detached from shafts and traces are being wound up.

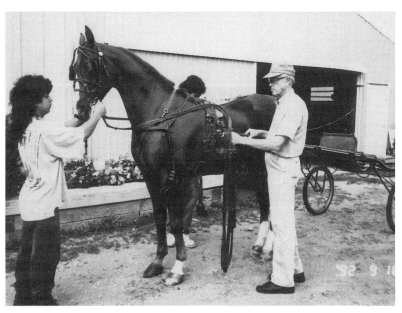

26B. Driver starting to push shafts back gently.

55

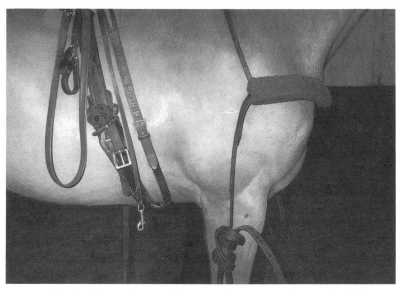

27A. Off side of horse, showing how martingale should be attached to harness saddle before removing. Note traces and safety girth knotted.

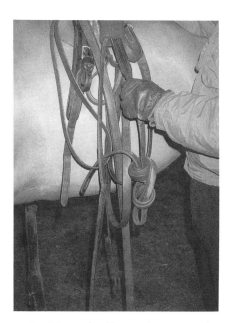

27B. Near side of horse, showing girth unbuckled and driver placing breastplate with traces behind harness saddle.

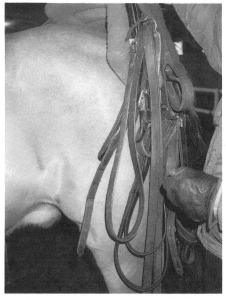

27C. Driver removing harness in one piece, being careful to remove crupper gently from underneath horse's tail.

28. Complete harness ready to hang up. Note that bridle has been hung over backstrap loop.

SUMMARY

With all due respect to those who can successfully put a harness right on a colt and hitch him to a drag, sled, bush, or other such contraption designed to acquaint him with driving and weight, we strongly advise adherence to the basic principles outlined in this chapter. Develop the colt slowly in his harness work. Admittedly, some horses will work out satisfactorily without this long bitting procedure, but they will never be as great a satisfaction to drive, both for manners and for style, as the horse that has learned to flex and set his head properly and to respond lightly to the bits.

In summary, here are a few basic rules to follow:

1. Take every step of training in order.
2. Be sure your equipment is of an appropriate type and will not break under stress.

29. For country driving, nothing can beat well-broken Morgans like this pair in Minnesota. Clifford Hitz is driving with his wife, Marilyn.

3. When the colt has done what you started out to teach him in a particular lesson, stop, no matter how short the working time has been.
4. Get help for hitching—and be sure the help you get is quiet but firm.
5. Remember: if the colt never learns to do anything wrong, he'll only know how to do things right (fig. 29).

CHAPTER 4

BREAKING THE COLT
TO RIDE

———•———

PRELIMINARY STEPS

Readers who are primarily interested in breaking a horse to ride rather than drive have probably turned directly to this chapter, eager to mount up. But are they ready to? The colt you plan to ride should be, at least, a very well developed two-year-old, or preferably three years old. Now, let's briefly review the preliminaries that should have been accomplished before commencing the colt's training under saddle:

First, the colt must be accustomed to his surroundings and must have been halter-broken and taught to lead and to be tied. He should have learned to accept wearing a sheet or blanket and having his feet trimmed or shod. (One is tempted to feel that if the colt has learned to be calm about all this it should be child's play to put on a saddle and bridle and start riding. Sometimes it indeed happens this way—if your colt is the one in a hundred who is absolutely unperturbed by anything—but it is unlikely that this kind of animal will ever have the necessary ambition to make a truly *responsive* show or pleasure mount.)

Furthermore, the colt should have been bitted and bridled, including work in side reins, and a check rein (overcheck or sidecheck) if desired. The bitting work prepares the mouth; the side and check reins help to place the head. Of course, it will be easier to guide the colt when you start to ride him if he already knows how to turn and responds to signals for starting and stopping. Accordingly, some work on the longe line and in long reins is also advisable before you ride. The longeing accustoms him to forward motion, the long reins make him calm in the bridle and handy in turns and stops.

Finally, the colt should be accustomed to the feel of a saddle on his back and of the bridle he will wear when he is ridden. Always place the saddle slowly and carefully well forward on the withers and then gently slip it back to the best position behind them. (Placing the saddle forward and sliding it back, rather than the reverse, keeps the hair of the back from rubbing the wrong way, which can upset even the best-trained of animals.) Move to the far side of the horse and adjust the girth slowly, being sure that the saddle skirts and flaps are smooth and the skin behind the forelegs is not pinched, then take up the girth on the near side with the same precautions. At this stage, do not attempt to tighten the girth as much as it should be for riding. If you have an old saddle, it is advisable to put it on the colt in the stall and leave it on him for a half hour or so for a couple of days, tying him to a stall ring so that he cannot attempt to roll with the saddle.

The first bridle should be a jointed snaffle, preferably the Deering style, although the half-cheek or plain ring snaffle is acceptable. First, slip the reins easily and quietly over the colt's head so that the buckle lies near the withers. Then put the bridle on slowly and carefully, holding the crownpiece in the right hand and the bit between the fingers of the left. Ease the thumb of your left hand gently into the upper left corner of the colt's mouth, making him open his mouth, then slip in the bit and work the crownpiece first over one ear and then the other. Then buckle the cavesson so that it fits neatly but not tightly about the nose, and buckle the throatlatch, allowing room for four fingers between the throat and the strap.

Most professionals like to start all young horses with a running martingale. Slip the neck yoke over the head and place it in front of the withers. Then, run the end of the martingale between the horse's front legs, and pass the girth through the loop and fasten it as usual. Take care to insure that the martingale fits squarely between the legs at the girth. Unbuckle the snaffle reins and run them through the rings of the martingale. Martingales are adjustable in length. The proper length may be measured approximately by setting the rings so that when you hold the reins back and up in riding position, they run in a straight line from bit to hand. The martingale is too short if the rings draw the reins downward from the mouth to hand position.

Two more things are worth doing before you prepare to ride the colt with saddle and bridle for the first time. It is a good idea to accustom him to things over and behind his head by holding an object up over his back as though a rider were mounted, or waving it gently above and behind his head. The youngster should also be introduced to weight. This may be done by leaning on him while grooming, laying as much weight as possible over him from the standing position, or better, by actually easing up onto the colt's back, lying across it, and gently petting him on both sides (fig. 30). One may ease a light person up on the colt bareback, provided the colt is not too nervous.

If all of these steps have been followed and the colt is responsive and willing, only one step remains before actually mounting

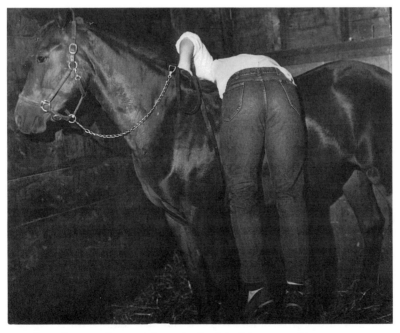

30. Introducing colt to weight on his back by lying across him.

him: to exercise him and let him work out any kinks before being ridden. Some colts can be turned loose for exercise; others may be longed, or put in the bitting harness and "worked down" until tired. The amount of pre-exercise will depend on the disposition of the colt. One that is extremely nervous or fresh, or one that is likely to be sulky and bullish, requires more work to make him safe for the first riding lesson. In questionable cases, it is better for the horse to be tired enough not to feel like bucking or running. It is not unusual for a professional to longe first and follow up with a good driving before riding the first ride, especially if he feels that the horse may be a problem.

MOUNTING

For the first mounting the colt's halter should be left on under the bridle. If an assistant is available, he can use the lead attached to the halter for added control. It will not hurt to lead the horse around at a walk and trot with the stirrups pulled down, flopping at his sides, for this will get him used to the feeling of more things moving about him (fig. 31). A few minutes of this will help him accept the rider's legs. If the mounting is to be done outside, it is best done in a confined area such as a ring or paddock. The rider must have heeled boots or high shoes and should wear protective headgear.

If the colt has taken all of this calmly, you may safely allow the assistant to go to the far side of the horse, hold the lead rein in his right hand, and grasp the stirrup leather in his left to steady the saddle as the colt is mounted. Stand at the colt's shoulder with the reins in your left hand, and the hand placed on the neck in front of the withers (and grasping the mane, if there is one). With your right hand, turn the stirrup for mounting as you place your left foot in the stirrup. Then, move your right hand across the middle of the saddle as you spring upward with most of the pull on your left hand. Your right leg should be carried clear over the horse's back and croup. Your right hand should be moved to the right front of the saddle to brace your weight, allowing you to land easily and lightly in the saddle rather than with a heavy thump (fig. 32). If the colt takes a step or two forward in the process, it is no cause for alarm. The assistant may then ease around in front of the colt and start leading him from the left side. After a few steps, if the colt seems nervous but not inclined

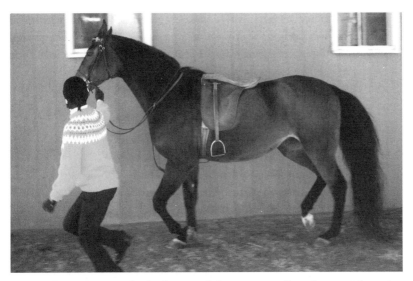

31. Before mounting, lead colt up and down at a walk and trot with stirrups down and flapping at colt's sides.

32. For first mounting, assistant holds colt as shown here by cheek piece, not bit, while grasping far stirrup firmly to prevent saddle from slipping around. Rider eases gently over colt's back with right hand braced to let weight down slowly. Assistant has stirrup turned so rider can easily slip foot into stirrup. 63

to run or buck, stop him and pet him. He may then be walked off again, with the assistant easing back and away a bit so that the rider takes control. The assistant should, however, remain in position to reassume control if necessary.

An alternate method should be used if the colt is expected to give trouble the first time. If you suspect that he may lunge, kick, buck, or even run backward, it is better to have the assistant stand on the near side by the colt's head. Keep the colt's head slightly to the left, and take up the reins with slight extra pressure on the left rein. Instruct the assistant to allow the colt to move off slowly after he is mounted, turning toward the left, and to continue to circle until you and colt are both settled to the new experience. This enables the assistant to effect a direct control, turning the colt in the one direction if he tries to lunge or run forward. The turning motion actually aids the rider's security and also protects the assistant from being kicked, since the head is turned toward him and the quarters away.

For the person who must mount without aid the first time, the preliminary work of leaning on the colt, lying up on his back, and even mounting bareback would be wise. If the colt is used to some weight and movement on his back without a saddle, he is less likely to be upset by similar procedures with the saddle. Even so, many trainers prefer to mount for the first time in the stall, where the horse is confined and also feels at home. Unless there is a fear of the colt's rearing or throwing himself, mounting in the stall the first time is very satisfactory, for pressure on the left rein while mounting will make him move toward the rider, and the colt has no chance to get loose. Once mounted, the rider can turn him about in the stall and walk him around both directions.

If the horse is kept in a straight stall it may be safer to find another place to mount the first time with a saddle. A small paddock is best. Here the colt can be faced into a corner and be surrounded, as it were, on three sides when the rider mounts. If no paddock is available, face him to a building, so that he is restricted in at least one direction.

Regardless of the method, it is wise to plan on circling the horse to the left for his first steps in motion. The forward and circling movement will help propel the rider into the saddle, will protect him from a kick, and will restrain the horse from leaping or running

out. If the colt has accepted the mounting and circling well, you can walk him about a few minutes before dismounting for the first time.

Dismounting should be done with the same care as mounting. Place the reins in your left hand and lay the hand on the withers. Place your right hand palm down on the pommel. Then lean your weight forward and upward until it is supported by your arms and left leg, remove your right foot from the stirrup, and swing your right leg carefully back, over, and clear of the horse's croup. Then, move your right hand to the back of the saddle so that you can support your weight on your arms while you free your left foot from the stirrup and let yourself gently down, free of the stirrups, eyes front in order to watch the colt. If there is an assistant, he may go to the off side, attach the lead rein, and hold the stirrup while the rider dismounts (fig. 33).

33. After the first ride, assistant once again holds colt and stirrup as rider dismounts slowly and carefully.

RIDING AT THE WALK

Although the colt's first few rides may be very informal sessions of mounting, walking, trotting, stopping, and dismounting for the main purpose of getting him used to a rider, the time comes for the systematic development of his different gaits, performed when and as desired by the rider.

The walk, the first of the three basic gaits, is more important than is generally supposed. For the pleasure or trail rider it is perhaps the most important gait of all, for more hours will be spent walking than trotting or cantering. Likewise, more importance is attached to the walk in a western or English pleasure or hack class than in the strictly show events, from a judge's standpoint.

When first ridden, a colt is apt to weave and wander instead of moving in a straight line. He is also likely to lower his head and extend it in order to balance the new weight, despite lessons in bitting harness, which may have produced a higher carriage. Too much should not be expected in early riding, for the colt must learn to balance himself under the weight of the rider, and if the rider is not light and expert in every way, the colt has that much greater a problem.

Whether one aims at pleasure riding or eventual showing, there is one habit to be prevented at all costs—jigging or jogging. This defense is adopted by many horses, and it is very fatiguing to the rider. The nervous jigging will cover less ground than a good walk or trot. Once a horse has gotten this habit, it is next to impossible to break it. Thus, the first step in training the horse at a walk is to encourage the long, regular, free steps that characterize the flat-footed walk. Many colts are sluggish and have to be urged into a stronger walk by voice encouragement and leg pressure. Light rein controls are all that are needed to keep the lazy horse from striding into a trot or jigging. The nervous or flighty animal, on the other hand, may want to trot or jig, or even canter, rather than walk. Here you must use great tact, for too much rein pressure will not only increase the colt's nervousness but incline him to jig anyway. This kind of mouth must be handled very quietly, with only light steady rein pressure to control increases in speed. A soothing voice and petting on the neck will do more to relax this type of horse and hold him to a walk than fighting him with the bit. Great patience must be exercised with a colt that is nervous and inclined to adopt a prancing gait at the start, for if he does not learn to relax and walk in his early training, he never will.

Once the horse has developed a good, strong, flat-footed walk, you can strive for the style desired for later showing. Flexion can gradually be achieved by urging the colt forward, while at the same time lightly resisting with the fingers. The moment the horse flexes a bit, the tension must be eased. In these basics at the walk the rider teaches his horse that he will "give" only when the horse yields, and resist whenever the horse "takes." This is the secret of getting a horse lightly "in hand"—to take until he submits and then give relief immediately. Keeping the horse up in hand by urging him into a proud head carriage with proper flexing will produce a more stylish walk with shorter steps. This collection makes a more handsome presentation for show horses, but is not suitable to the trail horse, western horse, or hunter, which all need a strong, ground-covering walk.

The horse destined for pleasure or trail riding needs more work on the walk as a developed gait than another type of horse, but the principles on which a good walk is developed are the same for any horse. Stumbling is a lazy habit for some and a result of adolescent awkwardness and "gawking" in others. It must be discouraged by keeping the colt well in hand and with his mind on his business. Work up and down hill is desirable for the young horse to be used for cross-country riding, as he needs muscular development to be a strong-going individual and give maximum pleasure to the rider.

THE TROT

As with the walk, the trot when first begun should be a free, natural gait; only later should the rider attempt to refine or correct the characteristics of the colt's trot.

A correct trot is well balanced, the horse's diagonal front and hind legs moving simultaneously. If the movements are not exactly simultaneous, there is likely to be a rolling motion that is uncomfortable to the rider and unpleasing to the eye. Along with the simultaneous action of the diagonal legs, one strives for a balance in the action of the front and hind legs: that is, a good square trot. There is nothing quite so uncomfortable and tiring to the rider as trying to

67

post to a horse that is moving quickly in front but lazily behind. The rider should post the correct diagonal when working in a ring or in circles. That is, when he is circling to the left he should be up out of the saddle when the colt's right foreleg (the outside leg on the circle) is up and forward. The opposite is true when the circle is to the right.

For the pleasure rider, the horse's action is judged more for smoothness than for appearance. Thus, it is very important that the pleasure animal possess a true trot. Remember that although it is the horse's second natural gait, most horses cannot attain great speed at the trot. The Standardbred horse is bred to trot at racing speed, and the five-gaited American Saddlebred can be pushed to considerable speed for the show ring, but these are not average "everyman" horses. Do not push your horse to trot too fast, as he will often develop either an uneven gait or a tendency to break into a canter when asked to trot.

For pleasure riding you can develop the trot in a natural way, without much concern for the exact head carriage and flexion demanded of the show horse. To urge the colt into a trot from a walk, you should shorten the reins slightly, thus signalling to the colt that something new is about to be asked. With the reins shortened, urge him forward with leg pressure, applied evenly on both sides, while relaxing the fingers on the reins to allow him to move his neck forward for balance as he begins to quicken his gait. You can also use your voice or a clucking sound to ask for more speed.

Notice that we advised first shortening the reins when about to change gait, and then, seemingly conversely, relaxing the fingers on the reins. The purpose of this is to attain a slightly shorter position on the reins for increased speeds with green colts. (The same procedure will be adopted in teaching the colt to canter.) In other words, the shortening of the reins will itself signal the colt to prepare for a change of gait.

To execute the trot, relax the rein tension enough to allow the colt to be impelled forward, either by leg pressures or voice urging. A steady hand is essential in these early lessons, for a colt is likely to weave some in direction and also to hesitate or spring forward faster. As he fumbles at the gait, much like a baby learning to walk, it is essential that the rider steady and support him but not discourage or impede him.

After the first few lessons in teaching the colt to obey the aids for the trot, you can begin to ask for a more finished performance. The aim is to develop a perfectly balanced trot with a steady speed, not a fast gait. The main consideration should be to keep the horse supple, steady, and correctly flexed. This can probably be done best at a medium or rather slow trot. Whether the colt is intended for pleasure or show, he should carry his head more or less perpendicular to the ground. In the pleasure horse, however, a lower carriage than that of the future show animal is acceptable.

Lessons should now continue with regular intervals of trotting, walking, and stopping. The rider should be patient but firm in striving to achieve perfect communication between himself and the horse, so that the gaits and stops will be smooth and graceful. It helps to vary the working areas somewhat so that the colt will not become bored.

For the colt (other than the one destined for a future in the sport-horse disciplines—see Introduction) that is destined for the show ring, the work at the trot, like the walk, must aim at proud and lofty bearing. More collection will be necessary to obtain the flexion and higher head carriage demanded for his future role. More propulsion is desirable so that the colt will appear to be really striving to go forward and yet be maintained in his gait by obedience to the rider's hands. In the early stages it is sometimes necessary to drive strongly forward with the legs, or even to use the artificial aid of a riding whip. It is important, however, to maintain perfect head carriage. The minute the colt responds with an eager trot forward, and at the same time sets his head at a good position, the rein tension must be relaxed enough to reward him for the compliance without abandoning it so far that he flounders into bad form.

In these early stages, while the trainer is still working with a snaffle bridle, he really predetermines whether the finished horse will be completely responsive to the bits and hands of his rider—whether he will be behind the bit, or be on the bit, or even "take the bit." The aim is to have him "on the bit" and responsive to it. At this point it is important that the horse be in hand; propelled forward by the rider's weight, legs, or voice aids; and instantly controlled in that forward movement, and his flexion and balancing to it, by submission to the rein pressures. Here, again, the rider's timing is of utmost importance. It is necessary for the rider to resist firmly as long as the horse tries to go forward and beyond the bit; but the instant the horse drops his chin to the pressure, the rider must immediately relax his hold and give to the horse. Again we come to the principle that the rider resists when the horse takes, and yields when the horse gives.

If the colt insists upon leaning on the bit and shows little sign of producing correct flexion after several weeks, you may switch to a twisted wire snaffle, which will be felt more sharply. You may then exert a gentle side-to-side, sawing motion to enforce compliance. The minute there is a sign of submission, the pressure should be relaxed. This sort of lesson continues until the colt learns the give-and-take principle.

A colt that gets behind the bit, on the other hand, dropping his head down and pulling his chin to his chest, needs to be driven forward steadily until there is a feel of his mouth on the bit. With this colt you may wish to switch to a snaffle bit with a leather or rubber mouthpiece, which will be softer on the bars of the mouth and make him more willing to accept the pressure.

THE CANTER

Although the canter is considered a natural gait, thorough control of the horse and considerable responsiveness between horse and rider are required for it to be executed properly. The canter is a three-beat gait, which starts with one hind leg on the ground in support, followed by the opposite hind leg and diagonal front leg in support, and finally the leading leg in front in final support. Thus there are two points in the three beats of the gait when only one leg is on the ground in support. A perfectly executed canter is collected, and the horse needs to have learned to collect himself properly at other gaits before he can be expected to perform a collected canter.

Because of all these factors, experienced trainers usually leave the canter until last. (In the case of a five-gaited horse, this may mean that he is already working in a full bridle and is almost ready to show at the other four gaits.)

Many professionals prefer to teach the canter with a full bridle because of the greater control and collection it affords. In addition, many horsemen insist that the canter be executed from a walk instead of a trot. (Most veteran show horses will canter only from a walk and will never fall into it from a trot because they have never been allowed to do so.) However, many fine pleasure horses, hacks, hunters, and western horses do move into a canter from a trot. For the inexperienced amateur struggling with his first colt, it may be easier and safer to teach the canter with a snaffle bit and allow the colt to jog a few steps into it, and to consider the perfectly executed, collected canter started from a walk as a goal toward which to work.

Begin by trying to produce a canter on the left lead—that is, with the near foreleg leading. This is the lead that you would use for a canter to the left, moving counterclockwise. To make the horse canter, a combination of aids—rein pressure to restrain him and flex him properly, and leg pressure (or whip if necessary) to provide propulsion forward. It is this combination of restraint and propulsion that produces the effort to canter.

Many different ways of combining restraint and energy are employed by various trainers and riders, but we will outline the one that we feel is most correct in theory and smoothest in execution. Remember, you are to take the left lead. First, increase rein tension slightly to produce flexion in the neck, the right wrist being bent to produce a bearing of the right rein, while the left hand remains stationary and steady to hold the head straight as the tension shifts the horse's weight to his right side. Sit completely erect and down firmly in the saddle, legs touching the sides of the horse in support, and ready for decisive movement. With your weight thus on the horse's right shoulder, wait until you can feel the left hind leg moving forward and down. At this point, press strongly with your right leg in support, back of the girth. Then, almost simultaneously, press the horse with both legs to force him up into the hands. The horse now has all weight on the right hind leg and moves up with all three other legs as the pressure is applied. Receive the horse up in hand, and ease tension so the horse may complete his first stride of the canter, while your fingers and wrists ease the head in its downward motion, ready to accept it in hand again on the next forward and upward stride (fig. 34).

In the second movement described above, the actual point at which you ask the horse to lift himself up into the canter, some people prefer to use the right leg against the horse's side behind the girth, and to nudge him on the left shoulder with the toe or tap it with the whip. Once the horse is properly positioned, with his weight on his right shoulder and side, you can feel when the right hind leg moves

34. Canter transition: Rider has just pushed horse into canter. Second beat of canter to left shows left hind and right front striking ground, with left foreleg to come to ground last for the third beat. (First beat of canter was right hind leg, which is already off ground.)

forward to support, and can exert energetic pressure forward at that moment to get the left lead.

No matter which way the horse circles, the weight must always be on his outside shoulder for the first position, and must have shifted to the outside hind leg when the rider demands the first stride of the canter from a walk.

The term "lead" is something of a misnomer, for the leading leg is actually the last to hit the ground in the three-beat sequence. Most riders tell which lead they are on by watching the horse's knee or his shoulder motion, but in time you should be able to sense it without looking down at all.

Experienced riders can readily tell by the balance and flexion of their horse the right moment to obtain the canter on either lead, and can tell just by the feel whether or not they have achieved the desired lead before the first stride is over. Occasionally a horse will become excited or so one-sided in his mouth that he will strive to strike off only on one particular lead. The experienced rider will restrain him long enough to balance him properly before allowing him to canter off on the lead desired.

For the amateur who is attempting to school his first horse, here are some suggestions that may work better for an inexperienced training hand.

First, shorten the reins enough to attain good collection and a feeling of control. This very shortening of the reins will indicate to the horse that you are beginning something different. Assuming that you wish to canter to the right, on the right lead, first exert pressure on the left rein, keeping your right hand steady, and push the horse forward with leg pressure. (If he takes a few steps at the trot, don't worry at this point.) Keep the rein tensions like this with greater pressure on the left, and keep pushing him with your legs until he bounces into the canter. When he breaks into the canter, ease off his head and do not try to produce too slow a canter at first. The worst error is to fall back on the horse's mouth when he begins the first stride, thus confusing him and causing him to trot. So ease off and let him canter at a fair pace for his first few times.

For green riders who have green colts that have not been brought along slowly through the various bitting processes, it is usually necessary to ask for the canter from a jog or trot rather than from a walk. To go from a trot into a canter on either lead, be sure you are posting on the correct diagonal, and place pressure on the rein toward the rail. Then kick with both heels to send the horse off into a canter. The combination of correct trotting signals and diagonals with body angle to the rail will almost always send the green horse off onto the correct lead.

Over a period of time the horse that learns to canter from the trot will begin to associate certain rein tensions and balance with the desired gait and lead, and learn to canter right from the walk. For the novice rider, the horse that can go gradually into the canter from the trot is usually easier to control and "rate" than the one that canters right from the walk.

No matter which method is used to teach the horse to canter, consistent work at the gait will eventually lead to almost instantaneous execution as soon as he feels the rider's touch on the reins. Horses that have been touched with the toe on the shoulder for the canter will often canter merely from this touch after repeated lessons, if the proper rein tensions and balance exist.

Actually horses learn to canter much by habit. There is one warning to be given here. If you are teaching the horse to canter and you are striving for a specific lead, do not jerk him to a stop if he picks up the wrong one. The rider's timing must be correct to get the correct lead. Never fight a colt for picking up the wrong lead or cross-cantering. When done correctly, the sequence of gait in a left-lead canter is (1) right hind, (2) left hind and right fore (diagonal pair), (3) left fore, also known as the leading foreleg. When a horse cross-canters the sequence becomes (1) right hind, (2) left hind and left fore (lateral pair), (3) right fore. Sometimes it is even wise with a nervous colt to allow him to canter incorrectly for a distance before bringing him to a stop and then restarting. Many horses have been spoiled by riders fighting them on the canter.

In riding at the canter the horseman strives to remain erect, absorbing the motion of the gait by relaxing his lower spine. It is essential that the rider have some give in his backbone to ride the gait well. Leaning forward too much will tend to pitch him toward the neck, while riding too far back or leaning back will produce a hollow in the loins and a pounding ride.

The motion of the horse in a collected canter is not unlike that of a merry-go-round horse. As the horse's forehand rises, the rider's body remains erect or rocks slightly forward on the buttocks; then it settles back again on the downward motion of the horse. The pitch of the saddle adds to the rider's motion, so the lighter and flatter the saddle, the smoother the gait will be to ride. The rider's seat should be smooth, hands steady, elbows in, legs still. Any serious flaws in form will tend to affect the hands and thus the composure of the colt.

Once the colt has begun to canter, let him stride along fairly freely while you allow him to attain confidence at the gait. Only then several sessions later, should you strive for more collection. A horse cantering with his head perfectly set in the bridle, light on the mouth, and at a slow, deliberate speed, is a delight to the eye and the rider.

The amount of tension required to put the horse into the canter will depend upon his disposition. For a very nervous animal only a very slight tension is required. Anything more may make him break into nervous bouncing or lunging before he begins to canter. Conversely, more placid horses usually require much more definite rein tension.

With horses that seem to pull or lug at the canter, the rider must resist the temptation to pull in return. Instead, he should try to push the horse forward with his legs or whip, to get his quarters under him, and raise his head. It is usually the lazy or awkward colt that seems to be about to fall on his face at the canter, lugging forward until it seems that the only thing holding him up is the bit. The idea is to tidy up the package, so to speak, by forcing the quarters up under him and the head and neck into greater flexion.

If the horse is difficult to slow down to a collected canter, work him in smaller and smaller circles. It may even be wise to put him back into the bitting harness and canter him in small circles on the longe. You can then drive the quarters forward from the ground with the whip while restraining him with the longe line and small circle.

EXERCISES FOR FLEXION AND OBEDIENCE

Throughout training under saddle, always remember that the colt must finish his lessons without being fatigued or bored. Thus, the length of the lesson may be determined not only by his performance but by his level of either fatigue or boredom. You may accomplish more in a ten-minute happy session than in an hour of boring repetition or tired resistance.

As already noted, the horse may quickly become bored with a day-by-day routine in the same place. Changes in exercises will help to relieve the monotony, but if you can employ not only changes in procedures but also in setting, such as hacking in a safe area, the horse will accept his training sessions more willingly.

Teaching the colt to back under saddle may properly come now, for this will add a fourth movement to the walk, trot, and canter already learned. First, you should be sure the colt will back easily from the ground. Facing the horse, take hold of the snaffle bit on each side and move it in a backward, alternating manner, while exerting pressure downward. The horse must learn to back with his head in a lowered position (fig. 35). Many people try to force a horse back by brute force, shoving his head high in the process. This places more weight on the hind quarters, which tends to immobilize them. Permitting the horse to drop his head lower will allow him to balance his weight on the shoulders and free his hindquarters to move. If the colt takes two steps backward the first time, that is enough. Reward him immediately with a pat on the neck, and lead him forward a step

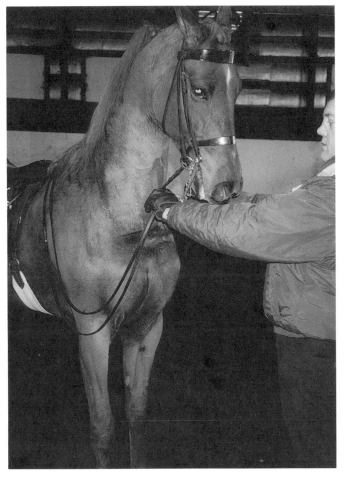

35. Teach horse to back up properly from ground before asking him to back while mounted. It is essential that the horse flexes his head back to the bit; if he resists, work at lowering head until he backs willingly.

or two. It is all right to repeat this two or three times in the first few lessons, but never ask for more than a few backing steps, or repeat it to the point of resentment. Backing (or the "rein-back") is very tiring to a horse.

Once the colt backs easily from the ground, you can try it from his back. Again it is best to ask only for two or three steps, and to reward the act with a pat and a chance to relax.

If your colt likes to rein back only too well, then there is no need to lower the head or to use much pressure. A tendency to back upon the slightest pressure on the bit should be discouraged. On the other hand, some horses refuse to back, either because it is awkward for them or from sheer stubbornness. One should not attack these horses with violent means to make them back; most will respond if handled quietly but firmly. Push back firmly on the bit from the front, at the same time simply stepping on the horse's own two front feet. He will usually lift a foot in the first movement, after which the pressure on his mouth will produce the backward motion.

For variety you may choose, on different days, to work on a straight line or in a ring. In ring work the routine can be broken up by making small circles about twenty-five feet in diameter at the corners at the walk, or about fifty feet in diameter at the trot. While working along the rail the colt should be required to move in a straight line. You should change the routines of work in the ring so that the colt is making circles at different gaits or at different places on various days. Be sure to circle as much to the right as to the left; avoid small circles that put strain on the horse's legs. In straight-line work the challenge is similar, but concentrate here on making small, neat, supple turns at the ends, and begin teaching the colt response and agility in tight situations. In each of these circumstances, ring or straightaway, the colt should be asked to walk, trot, stop, canter, and back, at various intervals and places. Remember to vary the sequence of gaits rather then always following the usual walk-trot-canter routine. Horses should not perform simply out of habit.

To check on the effectiveness of your work, it is fun to take the young horse to a completely strange area for work. This may be a neighbor's ring or a field down the road that he has not seen before. Practice the same maneuvers to see how well the colt pays attention to the rider and how quickly he responds when there are new sights and fascinations around him.

CHAPTER 5

FINISHING THE RIDING HORSE

•———

The riding horse discussed in this chapter is the horse destined for the show ring, not the sport horse, which is headed towards different riding activities. (We discussed the differences between the show-horse and the sport-horse disciplines in the Introduction.) The term "finishing the horse" may sound rather fatal, but it is just the customary term for what otherwise might be called "polishing," completing his normal education. For most horsemen this term is understood as training the horse to wear a full or double bridle, and in Saddle Horse parlance it includes the development of the two "extra" gaits, the slow gait and the rack.

BITTING IN THE FULL BRIDLE

Before we discuss introducing the curb bit and finally the full bridle to the colt, let us review the purposes of bits in the horse's mouth. Nothing is more essential to the horse's success than his mouth. If he is responsive to the bit, he will be happier as a pleasure horse and will certainly make his rider happy in the knowledge that he has perfect control. It is even more vital for the successful show horse to be properly mouthed. A horse cannot show with natural animation, brilliance, and action unless he is responsive to the bits and is a "happy horse" in his mouth.

Too many horses seen in the show rings exhibit an action produced more by anger and frustration than by any natural desire to trip along lightly and parade beautifully and cheerfully. Perhaps this is a sign of these times in which people are in a hurry for everything, and can't take the time to develop a light mouth and a happy horse. How much more impressive these same horses would be if they were traveling lightly in hand, eager and without fear of punishment on their mouths! Horses that are ridden hard up on the bit rarely work with their ears up, and usually they are seen fighting to open their mouths in order to lessen the bit pressure.

Until now, all work with the colt has been done with a snaffle bit. Any well-mouthed horse should be capable of being ridden in good form in a snaffle bridle. Until he has learned to carry his head properly and to flex lightly to the snaffle, he is not ready for a full bridle and the polishing that can be achieved with a curb bit.

The snaffle bit of the full bridle (also known as a double bridle) is used to raise the horse's head. It is also the balancing bit, which the rider uses to flex the horse's head for position or to adjust speed, and the bit from which the horse gains support from his rider.

Contrary to popular belief, the curb bit should not be regarded as a control measure, but rather as a flexing and polishing item. (Well-intentioned ringmasters and even judges may try to help a child who is overmounted by stopping him and tightening the curb chain on the horse; the result is sometimes seeing the same horse really throw a fit, taking off or rearing up, because the rider does not know how to handle the curb properly.)

The ordinary distinction is that the snaffle bit is used to raise the horse's head and the curb bit to lower and flex the jaw. While this statement is not entirely true, it is the easiest simplification for the amateur to grasp. A well-mouthed horse will flex to the snaffle and will also raise his head to it; he will flex his jaw even more to curb pressure. But while a well-broken horse will set his head perfectly when properly ridden on a curb bit, he may become excited or rear and lunge if a novice rider suddenly exerts unyielding pressure on it. So touch, feel, and timing become very important with this most useful of tools (fig. 36). For a further discussion of full bridles see page 116.

To teach a horse to wear the double bridle, it may be best to slip a bridle on with just a curb bit at first. If you have a curb bit with a

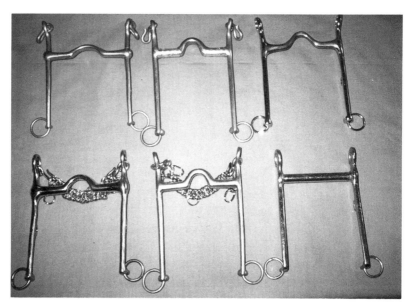

36. Six variations of a normal curb bit. Top row, left: mild port with short shank suitable for starting colt gently in full bridle and continuing on for pleasure. Middle: bit with longer shank, producing more leverage; it is best used by an experienced rider with good hands. Right: bit with medium shank, which has a light port comfortable for the show horse. Bottom row, left: heavier bit with medium shank, preferred by some, for a more finished horse. Middle: bit with higher port and longer shank, which may be preferred by experienced riders on strong-going horses. Right: straight bar. Occasionally one finds a horse that works best with this bit.

straight mouth, this is fine; otherwise, use a light curb with a low port. The bit should rest lightly in the mouth, just below the snaffle, yet above the tusks. It is important that the bit fit properly. One that is too narrow will pinch the sides of the mouth; one that is too wide will wiggle to one side of the mouth and may exert more pressure on the bars of the mouth on one side. After adjusting the bit in the horse's mouth, fasten the curb chain lightly. It must be flat and should not be too wide or too narrow, but should fit nicely in the groove beneath the horse's chin, just tight enough not to hang down on the lower lip.

Once the bit is in the horse's mouth and fitted properly, exert light pressure from the ground backward on the reins. As soon as the horse's jaw yields, immediately release the pressure (fig. 37). After a few exercises like this the colt or horse will learn that yielding with his chin relaxes the pressure. Occasionally one finds a colt that is so thick in the throttle and neck that he merely pushes out against the first pressures. In this case it may be helpful to push back on the bridge of his nose to help teach him to flex back to the bit pressure.

Take care to touch the curb rein very gently at first and to relieve the tension immediately when the colt responds so that he learns that his cooperation means relief. After this first introduction by the trainer, the curb bit may be employed with the bitting harness, but in a much different way from the process with snaffle or side reins.

Taking a simple bridle with a light curb bit, remove the reins and replace them with a piece of clothesline of the same length. Then get a small pulley, just big enough for the clothesline to pass through freely. The clothesline can be tied permanently to one ring of the curb, then passed through the pulley and fastened to the other curb ring. The bitting harness is put on in the usual fashion, and the curb bridle used in place of the regular bitting bridle. A small piece

37. Handler plays with the curb rein to teach flexion to the curb bit at will. Note response by horse.

of clothesline is needed to fasten the pulley to the check loop on the bitting harness. When this is first attached it should be loose and exert almost no pressure on the colt's mouth. Then move to the ring on the curb bit on the near side and gradually shorten the length of clothesline "rein" until it produces the flexion desired (fig. 38).

Using the pulley permits the clothesline rein to slide back and forth as the colt turns his head or moves about in the stall. He may thus move about freely while there is enough tension to produce flexion. As with the snaffle bitting harness, he soon "bits" himself. Do not leave him like this for more than ten minutes.

Never attach side reins to the curb bit rings in an unyielding manner. If something causes the colt to move his head quickly, the curb bit hits down hard on the bars and may make him rear or lunge, or even injure the bars of his mouth permanently.

The same procedure is followed with the bitting harness and curb bit pulley arrangement as with the side reins and the regular

38. Before riding with a full bridle, teach colt to wear the curb bit in the stall. Shown here is pulley arrangement described in text.

39. Properly fitted full bridle, also known as double bridle.

bitting bridle. Tension can gradually be increased until the horse willingly sets his head where it belongs. When he says "yes" by responding immediately to pressures without pushing against the bit, and keeps his mouth closed and relaxed, he is ready to be tried in the full bridle.

Proper adjustment of the full bridle is absolutely essential (fig. 39). The snaffle, or bridoon, should be fairly light, not big and bulky. It should be fitted so that it fits snugly against the corners of the horse's mouth but does not draw them up too tightly. Here again it is important that the bridoon be neither too narrow nor too wide. The curb bit should be above the tusks, below but not resting tightly against the snaffle. The chain should be hooked so that it does not fall below the horse's chin, yet is loose enough to permit placing two fingers beneath it. The chain should be laid flat, not twisted.

83

Once the bridle is fitted properly you should be able to stand in front of the colt and see that the snaffle is evenly drawn to the corners of the mouth on each side, with one-fourth to one-half inch of play between the rings of the bit and the sides of the head. In other words, the bit should be wide enough to permit a little movement from side to side without the rings hitting the mouth. The curb bit should rest just below the snaffle and should be no more than one-fourth inch wider than the mouth and properly balanced by the correct adjustment of the curb chain. (The upper shank of the curb bit above the mouthpiece should not pitch too far forward when pressure is exerted on the reins.)

This is a good time to do a little groundwork with the horse in his new full bridle arrangement.

A tall person may prefer to leave the reins back over the horse's neck and then to walk along beside him, holding the reins in proper riding position and "ride-driving" him from the ground. For any but the expert, groundwork with the new bits is safer than riding with them both the first time.

For actual first riding with the full bridle, use a martingale on the snaffle rein so that the horse can balance himself mostly on the snaffle, merely carrying the curb for feel. If the colt wears the full bridle without fussing, you can gradually work the curb bit in his mouth quietly for flexion, releasing the tension as soon as he responds. To use the martingale, lay the curb rein forward on the colt's neck in front of the martingale. Then pass the snaffle reins through the rings, which are held now outside the curb rein (fig. 40). The curb chain should be loose for the first lessons under saddle. The lessons should be short, and the flexing exercises mild. Now is the time to keep the colt happy and eager in his work, so do not fight him or demand too much. If you take time, and if your hands are light and "feeling," the colt will become a responsive individual whose head can be placed according to the rider's demands. Not every horse can set himself like a peacock, of course, but all will do a better job of carrying themselves, mouths closed and jaw relaxed, if the proper time and effort are spent in mouthing them from the start.

For the first work session under saddle with the full bridle, work only at the walk and trot. Do not attempt much speed at the outset. These first rides with the full bridle are only a time of acquaintance and preparation for the more precise demands that lie ahead.

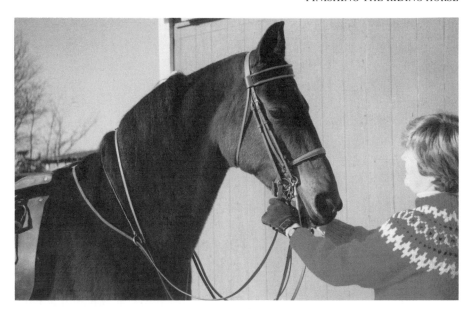

40. For the first rides with a full bridle, a running martingale should be used on the snaffle rein. When tacking up, put martingale on first, before bridle. After bridling, place curb rein forward on horse's neck; then unbuckle snaffle rein and run through the martingale rings on each side and rebuckle.

GAITING THE SADDLE HORSE

If the colt is to be "gaited," that is, trained to perform five gaits instead of the usual three, the first attempts should be made while the colt is still working in just a snaffle bridle, before he has been taught to canter. The main reason for this is that teaching a colt to do the unnatural gaits is problem enough without his knowing the canter as an additional defense.

Some people feel that they have a "natural" gaited horse if they have one that ambles, but this is not necessarily so. However, the future gaited horse must have a strong trot, and if he was not born with a good trot he must be taught. After the trot has been developed, as discussed in the previous chapter, the trainer may then think about teaching the colt to slow-gait or rack.

Gaiting a horse takes time and lots of patience, as well as a gifted hand with a horse. Some colts will start "hitting a lick" the first day the trainer tries; others may not do so at the rack for several weeks.

85

One of the best little gaited horses we ever knew did not take his first racking steps until after six months of trying. He went on to become a top gaited horse—but it took lots of time, sweat, and almost tears for the trainer to develop him.

So although we will explain the basic techniques used in gaiting a horse, we do not encourage any readers to attempt them unless they are experienced riders who have ridden at least a few five-gaited horses. Even in the professional show horse ranks there are comparatively few trainers who are experts in gaiting a horse. Many professional trainers can buy finished five-gaited horses and keep them in top shape, but few professionals are gifted in being able to actually gait a horse properly.

For ninety-nine per cent of the people who want a five-gaited horse, the best course is to send the colt to a professional trainer—and the choice should be a man who enjoys the reputation of being able to "make" a gaited horse. He will probably also be a successful showman in gaited circles, but not necessarily so. There are many top showmen who could not make a gaited horse although they could show one; on the other hand, there are "second men" or assistant trainers who could gait a colt beautifully but couldn't get around the ring at a horse show. So if you are going to have a colt gaited by a professional, take time in making the choice.

Nevertheless, everyone has to start somewhere to learn, so if the colt owner is a competent horseman, has ridden some gaited horses, and has a lot of "feel" from his fingers to his toes, then he may try gaiting his own and be successful. "Feeling" is vital to success in gaiting a horse, for you must know the feel of the gait and be able to tell when the colt is hitting a lick; you must be able to feel when he is reaching for a canter and to check him; and you must also know when to give, when to take, when to urge, and when to steady the colt and sit still in the saddle.

TEACHING THE RACK

The first step in teaching the horse to rack, oddly enough, is to call the blacksmith. The horse should be shod lightly in front with very little toe (some trainers start by racking them barefoot in front). It will help the colt to hit a lick of racking quicker if you leave the hind feet longer and change to a heavier shoe. This shortening and lightening in front, coupled with length and heavier weight behind, will unbalance him enough to help in learning the new gait.

Next, you will need quarter boots for the front feet. These may be regular quarter boots or rubber bell boots. If the colt is wobbly at all—and most of them are when learning the rack—shin and ankle boots will be a further protection, as he is likely to interfere in more ways than one in the process of learning to rack!

It is best if the colt is on the fresh side, unlike the earlier lessons, which are easier if he is settled. Bring him out fresh and try to find a slight downgrade to work on. If the spot can be found so that the colt can work downhill toward the stable, so much the better—he will be eager to go that way!

The colt should be wearing a snaffle bridle only. It is permissible to leave the martingale on, but you should pick the reins up in front of the martingale so that it will have no effect on the reins when you try to shake the colt up the first time (fig. 41).

Take the colt out fresh, walk him up the incline you have picked, and turn him around at the top. Now, as he is headed downhill (preferably toward the stable), shake his head from side to side with the snaffle reins. The reins must work in a sideways, not a backward, motion as you urge the colt forward (fig. 42). He will probably stop, wander all over the road, try to trot, or even bounce up into a canter. Very few will hit a lick of the rack on the first attempt. The idea is to throw your colt off balance so that he "scrambles" his legs under him to try to keep his feet as he goes downhill with his head swung from side to side. You are trying to break up his diagonal two-beat trotting gait and turn it into a scrambled one-two-three-four beat.

If you have the good fortune to get a lick of mixed gait in the first few attempts, quit and bring the colt to the barn while he is still fresh and eager. Another day is coming, and you will want the colt to be eager for the next lesson.

If the colt does not or will not hit anything but a pure trot or canter in the first few lessons, don't be discouraged. Keep trying as long as he is willing to go and does not become bored or tired. Probably thirty to forty-five minutes is the longest you should attempt to get him to hit a rack in any one day. You may either trot him back up the incline or walk him. If he has yet not ambled at all on the downgrade, it is useless to try to shake him going uphill.

Some horses will take to racking on absolutely level ground.

41. To start "shaking" colt into a mixed shuffle, rider holds the reins in front of the martingale rings to raise colt's head. By doing this, rider negates the effect of the martingale.

However, the downgrade is a help in most cases. Some horses can be shaken into the rack from a trot, and you can try this if the colt refuses to respond from a walk. However, it is preferable for him to learn this gait from the walk, as learning it from the trot may later cause complications at shows, where he may decide that racking is far more interesting than trotting.

It is important not to work the colt too long when he starts to rack—just a few steps in one lesson is enough. If he becomes too tired he may begin to pace (a two-beat lateral gait), and this is to be avoided at all costs. Don't ask the colt for speed in the early stages of the rack. A good four-beat gait, although slow, will be enough for now. Pushing him for speed too soon will encourage him to either shift to a pace or to run or half-canter behind. It is best to develop speed at his trot, and then gradually let him learn to go at speed in the rack.

42. First attempts at racking should be made on a downgrade; this rider also holds the reins in front of the martingale rings to raise horse's head.

If the colt still does not want to rack, one may add rattlers and chains behind (see Chapter 8) or switch to an even heavier shoe behind. The colt that is a pure trotter is best shod flat behind.

If, however, the colt shows an inclination to pace, the weight and foot in front should be increased, and the hind feet shortened and lightened. It may help to raise his heel behind and to square his toe. As with most training of horses, there is no hard-and-fast rule for racking a colt, and many different approaches can be tried. Racking is an artificial gait that must be developed over a period of time, and many switches in procedure may be necessary to produce the mixed gait. Some trainers pull the front shoes entirely to encourage the first "mixing."

Once you have the colt mixing a bit, he may then show some steady progress (fig. 43). However, this does not mean the colt will be gaited three months from the time he first started to rack. It is an exceptional gaited horse that does not require constant refreshing. There is always the tendency to shift over into a pace, or for others to slip into the trot. Some horses may resist the gait if away from it for any length of time and may jump up and down into a canter. So throughout his career it is likely the gaited horse will have to be worked by someone who knows the gait and how to keep it pure. This may result in changes of shoeing as the horse matures; indeed, the eventual show horse almost always goes later on with more foot and weight than he could possibly have started racking with in front.

Clever shifting of the rider's weight to balance the horse properly becomes essential. For the colt that tends to bob up and down into a left lead canter, the rider must shift his weight and that of the colt to the left, and turn the colt's head in the same direction, to inhibit the action. Many riders are inclined to make a colt one-sided on his mouth by pulling to that side unconsciously. Any of these tendencies mean that much more work to get a proper 1-2-3-4 mixed gait. The colt that is inclined to jump into one particular canter lead must be thrown off balance to make that lead impossible, while the colt that wants to trot only can be mixed most readily by a steady shifting of weight from side to side. Under no circumstances should the rider post when trying to rack the horse. The rider must sit down firmly and utilize his shifting weight to help scramble the horse's gait. Some of the best men at gaiting colts have been heavy men who lacked the finesse needed for showing a horse but had an un-

43. When colt starts mixing, rider resumes holding reins normally to let martingale help set horse's head.

canny ability to shift their weight and use their hands in the right way to mix up the horse's trotting gait.

It takes time to perfect the rack, just as it takes time and patience even to get it started. The colt receiving regular work can be expected to improve his form and speed over the course of the entire first year, and many will continue to improve for two or three years. Once the colt has the gait down well with the snaffle bridle, you can then proceed by refreshing his lessons in the bitting harness with the curb, and later start riding with the full bridle (fig. 44).

THE SLOW GAIT

The slow gait is known as a "stepping pace" in which the front legs move with an extremely hesitant motion while the hind legs bear the weight and control the speed. The horse steps distinctly behind, his left hind foot striking the ground just before the left front, and the right hind just before the right forefoot.

Occasionally one may teach a colt to slow-gait before racking

44. Once settled at the new gait, rider introduces the full bridle with a martingale used on the snaffle rein.

him. The procedure is the same except that no effort is made for speed. A horse with a very distinct, high trot may learn to slow-gait before he racks. Most horses, however, fumble around into the rack first.

To set the horse back into a slow gait requires much more elevation, and the horse is urged forward with legs, voice, or whip, while at the same time he is restricted from gaining speed. Extreme elevation helps to develop the high, exaggerated motion that is desired in this gait. The horse should pick each foot up deliberately and set it down with equal deliberation. In the slow gait he uses his rear end for propulsion, neither pushing up and under with his hindquarters as in the rack, nor stretching and flying out behind as in a fast rack. The slow gait should not be merely a slowed-down rack but should be a picturesque, high-motioned gait (fig. 45).

In describing the ideal slow gait, we must admit that it is rarely seen. Any who have seen some of the greats of the Saddle Horse world executing it will immediately recognize it, for once he has seen it in its perfection, a true Saddle Horse lover will never forget its beauty. The rare masters (and mistresses) of this gait perform it with all the bearing of a peacock, their heads high, necks flexed, eyes sparkling, ears forward, action high; and they seem to say, "Make way for royalty!"

45. At the slow gait or the rack, the feet hit the ground in four distinct beats. Here, the left foreleg is in support.

93

THE HAND GALLOP

For the pleasure rider or the hack class rider at shows, there remains the extended canter, or hand gallop. Mastery here is a case of respect between horse and rider and of responsiveness to the difference between the hand gallop and a runaway.

In the canter the horse was taught to carry his head high and neck well arched. Now in the hand gallop, he is released somewhat, his head and neck allowed to extend, so that he may flatten out to a shortened gallop.

In the hand gallop the rider should lean forward to balance the faster forward movement, pressing his legs to the horse for support so the hocks come well up under the horse's body. The hands should permit some extension of the neck for balance, but rein pressure should be maintained, more lightly but not dropped altogether. Thus the horse should be responsive to a request for a slowdown to canter or trot or walk. When brought down to a walk from the hand gallop, the horse should be given as much freedom of his head as possible to encourage him to walk in a relaxed fashion.

The hand gallop is the medium point between canter and full gallop. In the canter the horse is completely collected and under the rider's hand, while the full gallop employs the rider's hands merely as a support for the fully extended head and neck. The well-trained pleasure horse should be responsive and animated at all the gaits and provide his rider with an exhilarating but sensible ride.

SUMMARY

There is no quick method of producing a thoroughly pleasant, reliable mount. Work in the bitting harness is a prerequisite to riding to teach the colt responsiveness to the bit and give the future rider a chance to learn control methods. Driving in long lines is essential for a well-mouthed horse, whether or not he will eventually be driven in a cart. It is best to have your horse completely bridle-broken before he is ridden.

Be certain that the colt is used to handling from both sides, is amenable to things around him and contact from all directions, and is acquainted with the feel of some weight before he is mounted the first time. All steps of training require considerable advance preparation, and patience is the key word.

One cardinal rule should remain uppermost in any trainer's mind—*if the colt never learns to do anything wrong, he will make progress in only the right fashion.* The rule of caution, then, is to take the time to be sure nothing wrong happens. It is far easier, even if more time-consuming, to prevent problems than it is to cure them.

The colt that is rushed and "conquered" by a rough rider who sticks to whatever leaps or bounds the animal takes may eventually become a reliable mount; but he most assuredly will become a problem if in these first lessons his rider does not manage to stay on and the colt discovers that bucking, rearing, or whirling may dislodge the rider. So the sensible horseman strives to gentle the horse rather than enter into battle with what is, after all, an immensely strong animal. A person who feels that he has not the confidence or skill to master his colt, or whose colt is more highly strung than the average, is wise to give him to a professional whose skills are proven and reliable and who can green-break the colt for you.

For riding colts, or for that matter even aged horses, many experienced horsemen prefer always to carry a stick or whip of some kind. Usually this aid is not used, but it is far better to have it if needed than to need it and be without it. For early rides on colts, however, it is essential that the rider know how to use and carry the stick, for a wavering hand with a flapping whip will cause trouble. Therefore, we suggest a short stick or crop, not over twenty-four inches in length, as this will be easier to handle than the so-called "gaited whips," which are thirty or forty inches long and useful only to the expert.

For those intending to rack or slow-gait the colt, we want to emphasize again the need for much patience. If the colt is willing but is just not hitting a lick right, you may confer with an experienced gaited horse trainer for suggestions if you prefer to keep trying yourself. Once he is racking along fairly well, you can use the snaffle bridle with martingale to help get his head back into better position. The teaching of the rack has required raising his head and moving it from side to side to mix his gait; once it has been learned, the trainer must forget the rack for a time and work with snaffle and martingale to flex the head and neck again.

Working even the finished horse occasionally in just the snaffle

95

bridle with martingale is good therapy. Light winter training for the finished horse is also best done with alternative use of the martingale on the snaffle rein, even when you are riding with full bridle.

In breaking, always remember to check the adjustment of bits and bridle. If you have started with a young colt, his head may grow; if you have purchased a new bridle, the leather may stretch. Be sure to take the bit up evenly on both sides when dealing with the driving bridle or a bridle adjustable from the crownpiece. The cavesson of the full bridle should fit just below the cheek bones but well above the nostrils. Some horses work better with the curb chain used alone (the lip strap detached so the chain is allowed to ride higher under the jaw). These are adjustments that must constantly be tried and changed to suit the individual horse and rider.

CHAPTER 6

SHOW TECHNIQUES IN HARNESS

When we think of the harness show horse we automatically picture the high-stepping Hackney ponies or the elegant fine harness horses of today's show rings. They are joined by the other show pony types such as harness and roadster ponies, as well as by Morgans in harness, Standardbred in roadster events, and the various breeds and combinations eligible for pleasure driving competition.

We rarely see today the dignified style of driving that enhanced the road in coaching days or that graced our show rings in the early 1900s. In the heyday of fine driving, it was considered smartest and best to drive with the reins (also known as lines) in one hand. It made little difference to the expert reinsman whether he drove one, two, three, or four horses—he held the reins in his left hand and used the right merely for adjustment of the lines where necessary and direction of the whip as desired. The hand was held in the same position as in riding today, that is, thumb side up, with the elbow by the side and the arm carried so that the hand was at the center front of the body, the forearm horizontal. To turn right, the wrist was bent so that the thumb turned under and to the right; to turn left, the wrist was bent so that the little finger moved under and to the left. The right hand was kept ready to shorten or lengthen the reins or to use the whip. Adjustment of the reins by the right hand was done by placing the right hand in front of the left, not behind it.

When a "whip" (driver) used both hands, he still kept the hands close to each other and the body. The usual position of the reins was to carry them between the index and middle fingers, and this hold is preferred by the majority of reinsmen today, even though their arm positions vary considerably. Alternatively, some prefer to hold the driving reins much like a single snaffle rein, grasping the whole rein with one hand and allowing the bight to come up between the index and middle fingers, or between the index finger and the thumb. Another method used by some is to have one rein held with the full hold, and to have the other rein between the index and middle fingers. The final choice depends on the driver's own preference, coupled with the amount of hold needed to drive an individual horse.

A few general observations should be made regarding reins. The width and thickness of the reins you should use depend on the length of your fingers and the size of your hand. If gloves are worn, selection of the proper glove and fit are important. (It is best to wear the fingers a trifle long.)

The type of class in which you intend to show determines the type of harness and vehicle to be used. The rules are generally quite specific about this, but where some choice is possible, remember that a refined type of horse going in show classes appears best in light, neat harness. Certainly the harness must be appropriate to the vehicle. A road harness with breeching is acceptable with a road cart in pleasure classes but would not be right with a sulky or fine harness buggy.

In Hackney and harness pony classes as shown currently in the United States, overchecks are forbidden. The ponies are shown with a Liverpool bit and side-check. However, Hackney pleasure ponies are shown in a snaffle with choice of overcheck or side-check and with the martingale optional. Arabians may use either type of check, with a snaffle bit, the same rule applying for National Show Horses. The check style and bit are generally optional for Morgans. American Saddlebred fine-harness horses must have a snaffle bit with an overcheck (martingale expected). Roadster horses and ponies are shown in light harness with snaffle and overcheck (fig. 46), except that roadster wagon horses must have breeching. With other pony breeds, the bit and overcheck are apt to be optional. As you can see from all this, it is a good idea for anyone aiming toward a specific show division to keep current, as the rules of the American Horse Shows Association (AHSA) change constantly.

46. Champion Hackney roadster pony makes his winning pass out of the ring. This is Decision High Command, driven by Rick Wallen.

The best way to learn good driving is to sit next to an expert reinsman and watch his moves. The next best method is to watch expert drivers working at home or driving in the show ring. The novice driver should drive with the reins somewhat shorter than the expert. Driving with the reins too long can place the inexperienced driver in the awkward position of having his hands as high and far back as he can get them in a difficult situation, and still finding the situation impossible to control. It is best to drive with the upper arms down at the sides or slightly forward and the forearms parallel to the ground rather than lifted upward into a tiring position. It is also best to drive with the hands close together, so that you can quickly reach for the reins to shorten them as necessary. A steady hand is essential, as the horse in harness responds very quickly to directional bearings, and the novice can easily find himself weaving a serpentine pattern. A slight movement of the wrist will usually turn the horse quickly enough in the show ring.

Always check the harness and bridle carefully before getting into the vehicle. Be sure the traces are adjusted so the pressure of pulling is upon them; push the cart or buggy back so the traces are taut as you wrap the safety strap. Then there will be no flapping traces indicating that the horse is pulling the vehicle via the reins! Be sure the bit is adjusted properly and the check rein is the proper length. The martingale, if used, must be properly set also. Always have the reins in your hand from the moment the horse is hitched, carrying them with you into the cart or buggy; never get into the vehicle and wait for someone else to hand you the reins. Once in the vehicle, signal your groom or helper when you are ready to move. Shorten your reins and feel them lightly so the horse knows that action is about to begin. With a nervous horse it is best to wait until you are ready to move, or have moved the first few steps, before having the check rein attached. It is always a good idea to make sure this horse wears his check comfortably while standing, first.

One of the hazards of driving is the chance that a horse will swish his tail and get it over a line. If this happens, don't pull on the line; rather, try to loosen it and urge him forward with the whip so that he raises his tail and allows the reins to come free. Pulling on the line upsets the horse's mouth, increases pressure on his tail, and can cause him to kick or otherwise misbehave. If he does not relax his tail and allow the line to come loose, bring him to a stop and then lift his tail off the rein—don't pull the rein out from under his tail. This problem almost never occurs with Saddlebreds or show ponies with set tails, but it can be bothersome with horses that are free to swish their natural tails.

When you enter the show ring in competition, you have other horses and vehicles to consider (fig. 47). Allowance must be made for wheel clearance in passing or being passed. The best position for showing is on the rail, by yourself. Sometimes it is necessary to cut a corner to position oneself, or even to drive across the ring, but once a good spot is found on the rail it is generally best to keep it, for the horse will work more steadily on the larger circle with the rail for guidance. Occasionally a class is so large that circling on the inside is necessary, either to be seen or to be safe. Generally, however, the safest and most effective position is on the rail with ample space in front of you. Judges prefer the expert who can place his horse well and show him to best advantage from the rail position. A horse that is cutting around the inside cannot be seen as steadily or objectively by the judge as one that is moving straight along the outer rail.

When asked to line up, the driver should allow for good spacing between vehicles and remain alert to his own horse and those around him, as quick movement may be necessary to avoid an accident. In many classes a helper is allowed to come into the ring and head a horse in harness events. A horse that is nervous and won't stand is better walked about than forced to stand and perhaps throw himself. Many horses will stand unchecked but will not stand quietly with the check rein up high. This is something to consider when checking the horse.

As in all classes at a horse show, any driving class requires poise and thought on the part of the driver. He should sit erectly but not stiffly, handling the reins in the fashion most effective and easiest for him. Exhibitions of drivers leaning far to one side, with one hand held low and the other high and wide, are just that—exhibitions.

47. A three-year-old making its first show is broke well enough for driver to control its natural desire to shy off at strange sights.

101

The most discreet drivers handle their lines with dignity and without lavish arm-waving (fig. 48). For the novice driver, careful, steady driving is essential. Women are particularly prone to feeling a need to raise their arms from the elbows for a stylish appearance. This is not necessary and weakens their effectiveness in handling the lines, as the raised position tires the hands and makes them less responsive to the horse's mouth.

Many means are employed by professionals to develop more trot in harness, either for action or for speed. We discuss these additional training methods (some of which may be seen at today's horse shows) in some detail in chapter 8. Briefly, however, chains, rattlers, and developers are the commonest devices, along with the quarter boots that are regularly worn by fine harness and roadster entries. Most amateurs can safely experiment with chains and rattlers and can quite safely use quarter boots. Another training device—shackles—is used by some professional trainers. Some top horsemen refrain from using shackles, however, as they usually mark a horse with an artificial movement that is instantly spotted by the expert judge.

Chains may be worn in the stall as well as during working hours, but rattlers should be used only during training periods. Some horses respond best to chains behind and rattlers in front. With others, the reverse works, so this is something to experiment with. Some horses take a few exaggerated steps when the gadgets are first added and then resort to their usual way of moving. Others respond very well to the added aids. When using chains or rattlers, make sure that they do not chafe the horse. Some horses are thin-skinned, and their coronets or pasterns may become sore from the movement of chains or even rattlers.

If a horse lacks high action in his trot up front, toe may be added, as well as weight. Generally, a toe-weight shoe will encourage him to roll his shoulders and reach farther; a heel-weight shoe will usually encourage him to fold his legs up under himself more quickly. A long toe generally increases stride and action, but care must be taken to be sure that the heel is proportionately high so the horse has good support for his tendons. On the other hand, too high a heel may cause a horse to go choppily. Once you find an ideal movement for your horse, it is a good idea to take the angle of his feet and attempt to keep him at this same angle in later shoeings. Angle can have more to do with his way of moving than a half inch more or less of

48. A finished Saddlebred fine-harness champion: Royal Crest Sandstone, driven by Rick Wallen.

foot. Remember, long feet and weight will increase his stride and action, but they will also shorten his years of soundness. Here the owner must choose whether to go all out for the greatest performance today, or take his time to develop a pleasing performer that may last much longer.

Handholds are much used today. These are a great aid to women and children in driving and are also used by many men. They must be properly adjusted so that they are in the right driving position when the horse is performing at the trot. This means that the driver usually must hold his hands well forward when walking or stopped.

Discretion is necessary in the use of the whip while driving. If a horse is at all inclined to kick, the whip should be used only in front of the saddle and girth. Occasionally it can be used effectively to help a green colt turn—tapping him on the right side to turn him to the left, and so forth.

Improper checking of horses is one of the commonest faults at horse shows. The horse should be checked only high enough to perfect his head carriage at a well-flexed position. Some horses are checked so high that they cannot set their heads and go at a well-balanced trot but are forced back on their hocks instead. The only excuse for extreme checking is danger that a horse will kick. For the horse that is likely to kick, higher checking may be advisable to avoid the danger, but it does have drawbacks, chief of which are loss of comfortable free motion and his unwillingness to stand still when stopped.

CHAPTER 7

SHOW TECHNIQUES
UNDER SADDLE

---·---

THE SHOW HORSE

Before discussing specific show techniques for the show horse (as shown in park, gaited, and pleasure classes—see the differences between what we call show horses and sport horses in the Introduction), let us consider just what showing a horse constitutes and what attributes a show horse must have. For some, showing a horse means nothing more than paying an entry fee and putting the horse in competition in the hope of winning a prize. To others, showing means a spectacle, and that may be characterized by a wild-going horse and a dashing rider, a combination that catches the eyes of spectators but does not register in the prize awards. For the experienced show-goer, the connoisseur of good horses and good showing of them, a horse show involves the exhibition of quality horses, presented in an effective yet dignified manner, performing in the finest form possible for their given class.

Whatever division one fancies, "personality" is a vital factor to a show horse. The best show horses have abundant breed type and quality for their division—an aristocratic look that sets them apart from the ordinary. Their action should be eye-catching but perfect in balance and form, as high as possible in some breeds, yet without achieving this height of action at the sacrifice of form and grace. In other breeds height of action is not valued as such, and the emphasis is on a symmetrical, straight, true movement of the legs. In whatever division or breed one competes, the action must be balanced and even, the hocks moving in perfect synchronization with the forelegs. There is an old saying among Saddle Horse trainers that "a show horse must have his head up, his ears up, and his tail up" (fig. 49). If he has all the action in the world, but lacks any of these details, he fails as a show horse.

In showing, one always strives for perfection. That endeavor starts with a beautiful animal, continues through patient training, develops through the advancement of rider with horse, and culminates in precise, animated, but mannerly performances in the horse show ring. The show horse must be well-mannered to perform all the routines required of him cheerfully and promptly. Occasionally a bad-mannered horse proves spectacular and successful for one particularly talented trainer, but this is an exception. The best trainers cherish most the horse that is eager and ready to show, yet perfectly responsive and obedient to every command. This ideal type of horse can be put in whatever notch the rider wishes, ready to give every ounce of his ability when called upon.

Manners being so necessary, it follows that these manners must be cultivated from the earliest days of training. The horse should be approached with kindness, yet the trainer must be firm in demanding obedience at the proper times. Little habits that may seem cute when the colt is young, such as nibbling at the buttons on one's jacket, can become dangerous problems when the horse is full grown. The owner does the colt a favor by establishing firm discipline at the very start. It will make life easier for the horse and for those associated with him for the rest of his life, for you must remember that the horse is a creature of habit—and if you let him get into bad habits, someone must later attempt to break them.

Thus, the manner in which the trainer brings his colt along, combining kindness as daily fare with discipline as necessary, will be reflected in that horse's acceptance of his role in life and even may be reflected in his obvious delight in showing off. There are horses that definitely love to show off, that are regular "hams" when they have an audience. They have learned to obey commands but have received enough plaudits (if only a pat on the neck and a kind word) for their performances to sparkle before an audience.

49. *Rick Wallen showing Callaway's Mr. Republican, a five-gaited World Champion American Saddlebred with "his head up, his ears up, and his tail up."*

If the horse is to perform in the show ring with presence, that ears-up appearance, he must be relaxed and happy. As horses display much of their personality through their ears and eyes, it is essential that these be alert and confident rather than turned or rolled back in fearful anxiety or sullen anger because the rider is impeding the horse's performance (fig. 50). And impeding is just what many riders do when they believe they are "helping" the horse. Jarring, heavy hands on the horse's mouth, spurs in the sides, or whip slapping at the sides or over the ears—all of these maneuvers can be upsetting to the horse, causing anxiety to some and anger in others.

The show horse must be eager and animated and look ready to jump out of the ring at any moment, yet be perfectly responsive to the rider's commands. He can be so only when properly mouthed, properly schooled and mannered, and then beautifully ridden. The challenge of this field of showing is unequalled, and only those who have tried all fields can truly appreciate the exhilarating joy that comes to a rider on a horse that is doing his all and delighting the railbirds with his presence every step of the way. Few have the privilege of riding those rare "greats" of the show horse world; many more people, however, have the privilege of seeing them in action and of sensing the ecstasy of a fine rider feeling a great mount move beneath him.

So let us consider some contributions the rider may make to help his horse show with ease and presence. Since little actual grip is necessary to stay on a "broke" horse that is ready for the show ring, the lower leg may fall naturally to the stirrup and away from the horse's sides. Nudging lower legs can divert the horse's attention just as much as a flapping whip. The ideal situation is for the rider to remain as motionless in the saddle as possible, his legs still, his seat close to the saddle, his hands quiet and flexible. Remember, the object is to let the horse show off without impediment, so the rider should try to avoid distracting him with worries about what is kicking or slapping at him, or what is pounding on his back, or what is jabbing him on the mouth. It takes a game horse to show well under the abuse that many riders heap upon them in the mistaken idea that they are "helping" the horse.

One of the most common fallacies, or abuses, that we see in the show ring is the all-too-common practice of driving the horse madly up onto the bit, taking a death grip on the reins, and forcing the horse to lean on the rider. Often people will complain that a really perfectly mouthed horse "just won't get on the bit." A horse with a good mouth that is ridden by someone who knows how to handle him will set himself perfectly in the bridle, often with the reins only occasionally taut to place his head in position, then slacked to permit him to parade like a peacock, ears up, and looking with sparkling interest at the world around him.

An abuse that goes with the first is driving the horse constantly with the spurs in his sides or with a whip swished over his ears. Under these conditions it is impossible for a horse to show off by looking at

50. A champion Morgan park horse, Topfield's Janet, being shown going in a happy, relaxed way by Carl Childs. This horse was trained without the use of any of the devices discussed in the next chapter.

109

the crowd; he is too busy worrying about the next gouge or the next slap over his ears!

A third abuse is seen most often at small shows in riders who, having heard that bouncing on the horse's loins will produce more hock action, sit on the cantle and really pound away at the horse's kidneys. Indeed, there may be more action of some kind, but it is unlikely to be the proper type of synchronized motion. These same riders often lean back and ride with their feet "up on the dashboard."

To show a show horse in really fine form, one must do everything possible to encourage him to show freely and to be eager and interested in the things around him. The rider is there to place him where he needs to be in the ring, to help him change gears at the judge's command, and to guide him in showing off. Before entering the ring the rider must double-check to be sure that the saddle is placed properly and the girth cinched properly; he must be sure that the bridle is properly adjusted and that all straps are down in the keepers; he will be sure that the horse's hoofs are clean, that forelocks or braids are in proper place, and that the muzzle and mouth are clean. After making sure that the horse is in top condition for ring entry, he must check himself to be certain that his tie is straight, his hold-down straps under his instep, his hat straight, his reins well adjusted, and his whip, if carried, quietly in place.

Most classes enter the ring and circle to the left, counter-clockwise, and are expected to enter at a trot. It is a mark of inexperience to dash through the gate with several other riders in a cluster. Yet even in classes with only five or six competitors, one often sees several constantly bunched together, while only one or two ride wisely off by themselves. Start using your head right from your very entry into the ring. Never follow right on the heels of another horse; give him room to enter and start around before you make your entry. If there are ten horses trotting in a line right ahead inside the gate, it is only common sense to cut diagonally across the ring and seek a spot with less traffic. From the time of entry until the class has completed its work, the rider should always strive for a good position, on the rail wherever possible and without horses close up if possible. In a very large class it may be necessary to pass or even to ride inside, off the rail, for a while; but even in large classes the best riders seek a good location on the rail and let the novices do the cavorting in the infield.

Throughout the class, be ready for commands and execute them as soon as is possible or practicable. But if you are trotting and the command comes to walk just as you are approaching a horse that is being hauled to a sudden stop, it is best to continue trotting past and then pull your horse to a walk. If you are cantering and hear another horse thundering up behind on your tail, it is best to continue after the command to walk so that you are out of the other horse's way. If you are riding a particularly electrifying animal at the trot and the command to walk comes just as you are approaching the judge, it is permissible (and smart) to continue down the rail past the judge before coming to a walk. Knowing how to operate in a class and when to make moves is known as "ring presence" and is something that comes from experience in showing. But as with so many aspects of work with horses, most of it just amounts to common sense and good judgment.

When the command comes to line up, use some judgment in selecting your position. It is best not to join in a mad dash for the center where the judge and ringmaster are standing. Try to select a position that is comfortably away from other horses but not at the extreme end of the ring where the judge must walk extra steps to find you. If you are showing a stallion, of course, it is best to line up at the end or to leave ample space between horses. The judge will appreciate exhibitors who line up promptly somewhere near the center, yet leave room enough for him to walk between the horses comfortably. When the judge approaches, the exhibitor should be mannerly, speaking only if spoken to, or smiling an acknowledgment if the judge comments pleasantly about the horse. The exhibitor should not speak to the judge in the ring unless spoken to first. The only exceptions are emergencies or, in individual performances, when the rider may properly ask the judge for clarification of the requirements.

For the amateur it can be very helpful to have a friend or trainer outside on the rail to assist with suggestions in first shows. Until the rider is experienced he may lack the knowledge to feel when his horse is at the right speed, or when his head needs to be raised, or when he needs to drop his chin.

One should strive to ride with poise throughout a class. Even when little things go wrong, such as taking the wrong lead at the canter, the rider must strive to look calm and in command of the situation, and promptly correct the mistake without a lot of fuss in the ring. Movements of the best riders are nearly imperceptible to judge

111

or spectators; their performances are polished by a poise and ring presence that comes to most with experience in the rings. For a few this poise and presence seems to come naturally, just as it does to some horses; for most of us it must be learned and cultivated (fig. 51).

In contrast to the park or gaited classes, in which one wants a horse to have ears up, eyes alert, and an "about-to-explode" appearance, the pleasure classes require above all that the horse appear reliable and a pleasure to own and use. If he can give the appearance of absolute dependability and at the same time work with his ears eagerly up, so much the better. But here one does not want the eyes to sparkle with excitement nor the action to appear so high and exciting as to be taxing to either horse or rider. When pleasure-horse performance is being judged, the prime requisite is perfection of manners. The horse must be responsive to the rider's slightest wish, willing to move out faster when asked and just as willing to slow down, stop, or stand still at the lightest touch.

Riding the pleasure horse "on the buckle" (that is, with reins held way out at the end, so that there is no contact with the horse's mouth) has gone out of style for all English pleasure breed classes, although riding with the reins really loose is still "in" for western pleasure. Most pleasure classes call for light contact with the horse's mouth, and many judges have no objection to a collected ride, provided that the horse exhibits a light mouth and a highly responsive attitude. It is useless to ride with the outside reins (away from the judge) held rather short while the inside reins lie slack. The judge can easily spot this tactic and will not be impressed. A good judge will also see the horse that does all his gaits on a completely loose rein but that puts his nose up, against the bit, when the command to walk or stop is given.

One must consider the breed division as well as the abilities and responsiveness of the individual mount to decide just how loose the reins or how collected the horse should be. The general aim should be to present the pleasantest possible picture to the judge—a rider having a smooth, comfortable, happy ride on a horse that is perfectly responsive to any command.

Vital to any pleasure horse is a good walk. Some judges will make their final decision on this gait alone, for the walk is a basic pleasure gait; there can be no pleasure in riding a horse that does not have a good, ground-covering flat walk. Any tendency to jig or jog, to move

112

51. Desiree Devries, an amateur rider-trainer, showing J.M.F. Debbie Beam with poise and presence.

sideways, or to start and stop is seriously faulted. The rider must spend plenty of time in developing this gait and then show his horse in the ring with a manner that indicates absolute faith in the horse's willingness to walk along in mannerly fashion all day long. The rider himself must be relaxed, sitting down and slightly back in the saddle at this gait.

The trot may be called for in various speeds. If the rider expects to be asked for an extended trot (at speed), then he should restrain his horse to a normal trot until the command comes for the extended trot. But while speed is looked for at the extended trot, it is also important for the rider to sense the point at which his horse begins to lose form and balance. The rider must rate his horse and call for the extended speed only to the point at which the horse can move off squarely and well. Pushing him to the breaking point will quickly eliminate the horse from consideration. Some horses will interfere

113

when pushed beyond their normal limits for speed. Care should be taken to keep the horse at the speed he can go well, in form.

Like the trot, the canter may involve variations in speed in pleasure divisions. A judge may ask for a slow, collected canter; he may ask for just a regular canter; or he may ask for a hand gallop. The hand gallop is an extended form of the canter and requires just what the terminology suggests—a gallop that is "in hand" and not just a flat run. A horse that shows often in these classes may anticipate the command to move on at speed. The highly rated horse will canter slowly and lightly as long as the rider wishes.

In pleasure classes, it is wise to use changes of body and hand position that instantly telegraph to the horse the change of gait or speed. A variety of methods may be used to suit the individual rider and horse, for in time a horse can react to whatever signals the rider adopts, provided they are consistent in application. Some successful riders will sit the trot and not post during the slow or jog trot; almost all riders rightly incline their bodies forward and take a steadying hold on the reins for the extended trot. For the canter most riders sit easily erect with just a light touch on the reins; for the hand gallop a forward inclination of the body is proper, buttocks up off the saddle, and a shorter rein for control of speed, especially on the turns.

As with the park or gaited horse, the less the rider badgers his horse, the more willing and happy the horse will look. The rider should place his horse well, on the rail wherever possible, but move inside so the judge can see him if the class is large and crowded, as many pleasure events tend to be.

The overall impression the judge receives is all-important. He must feel that the rider is having a perfectly pleasing, relaxing ride. He must feel that the horse is obedient, willing, able, eager, and also attractive. After all, one who has a pleasure horse wants him to be a pretty animal, too. The manners come first, but a beautiful horse has an edge over a plain one when the chips are down.

THE RIDER'S CONTRIBUTION

In any saddle classes the taste of the owner or rider in selecting tack for the horse and apparel for himself becomes important. The "forward-seat" jumping saddle, ideal for the hunt field or for straight jumping (sport horse activities), is a poor choice for any type of showing in the ring where action of the horse and breed conformation are to be judged. The jumping saddle fits up over the horse's shoulders, hiding much of the beauty of the shoulder conformation and action of even the best horses. For strictly show breeds, the popular choice is a show saddle with cut-back head and cut-back, wide skirt (fig. 52). This allows maximum shoulder movement, sets well back of the withers, and provides protection to the rider's legs, which are usually straighter in this style of saddle than in others. If one wants a good saddle for shows but also needs to use it for cross-country riding, the choice may be a good close-contact or polo saddle (fig. 53A & B). The fairly flat seat of this saddle places the

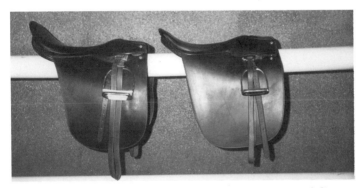

52. Cut-back show saddles come with a deeper equitation seat (left) or a normal flat seat (right).

A.   B.

53A & B. Close-contact saddle (A); polo saddle (B). The best choices for a general purpose saddle.

rider near the middle, instead of back, as in the cut-back show saddle, and the skirt is cut only slightly forward from the pommel. This saddle is comfortable for pleasure and trail riding but light and acceptable for showing.

The choice of bridle depends on the horse and the type of classes he will enter. For most horses the full bridle, with snaffle and curb bits, is the choice (fig. 54). The selection of bits is important, as discussed earlier. They must fit the horse. The most popular style of cavesson is the plain stitched leather, narrow style, although many today favor a colored cavesson to match the browband, this also being narrower than the browband. The color of browband and its width are optional; some riders like to have the browband match their own riding habits, for example. In pleasure classes you should avoid a curb bit with a long shank, and most certainly you should avoid having an extremely tight curb chain. (Some judges will feel for the tension

54. Four combinations of snaffle and curb bits that may be found in full show bridles. From left: high port curb bit; snaffle with very mild curb bit; twisted wire snaffle with sliding cheek bit; heavier twisted snaffle with mild curb bit wrapped with wire. Note that a lip chain is not used on second and third bridles.

here.) In many pleasure classes it is permissible to ride with a plain snaffle (no martingale), but this is not proper with a cut-back show saddle.

The appointments—that is, saddle and bridle—must go together. A cut-back show saddle always calls for a full show bridle. With this combination the rider should select clothes to complement his tack— a full saddle suit. If the rider elects to use a hacking saddle with a full bridle in pleasure classes, he may be a bit more informal and wear saddle jodhpurs with a conservative, if contrasting, saddle style coat. If the rider chooses to use a hacking saddle, or a forward-seat style saddle, with a snaffle bridle in a pleasure event, he may then quite properly wear hunting clothes, such as breeches, boots, and an appropriate riding coat. One should consult appropriate breed manuals or rule books for specific regulations on dress, as conventions change often.

The appearance of the horse and rider as a combination should be congruous. Just as the clothes and tack must match, so must the style of riding. An excellent saddle-seat rider in a fine saddle suit would be out of place riding a horse with a forward-seat saddle and snaffle bridle. Likewise, the good hunt-seat rider with hunt clothes would appear ridiculous on a cut-back show saddle. The combination of horse, tack, rider's apparel, and rider's style of riding must fit together to make a balanced, attractive picture.

Suitability of the horse for the showing tasks required of him is essential. The rider's ability to present his horse adequately will improve with time, experience, and astute observation of the competitors who win. Many of the breeds normally shown under English tack are now doubling into the western pleasure classes, where western equipment and attire are essential.

SUMMARY

The word "show" may bring to mind the act of demonstration or a brilliant display of beauty for the entertainment of spectators. However one views the word, we must recognize that a horse show requires both horse and rider or driver to appear at their very best.

Training that emphasizes the mannerly development of responses suitable to his breed and class requirements is essential to success for any horse headed for the show ring. All the ability in the world will not bring show ring success unless that ability is trained and channeled in the proper direction and can be controlled.

Conditioning is a second requisite for success in the show ring—and this conditioning includes not only exercise and muscling for performance but also the grooming and feeding that are essential to healthy growth, happy disposition, and gleaming coats.

Presentation of the horse, already trained and properly conditioned, becomes all-important on the actual day of showing. Taste in the selection of equipment for showing, judgment in selecting the proper classes and then in making the entry through the gate, dedication to making the best performance possible while in the ring from start to finish of the event, good manners and good sportsmanship on the part of the showman—all these things contribute to the overall impression made in the presentation of the horse.

To be successful in the show world a person must first love horses, then be willing to work hard for perfection in himself and his mount; he must respect people and recognize variations in personalities; and he must be game enough to keep striving for perfection, to accept defeats gracefully, to profit from the example of others, to recognize his own deficiencies, and to keep trying. Finally, a person must be able to lose, and also to win, with a smile.

CHAPTER 8

TRAINING DEVICES AND SHOEING FOR SHOW HORSES

•

In this chapter, we will first deal with the most common training aids used (and sometimes abused) by some professional trainers throughout the country. These may be seen in the working and warm-up areas at horse shows. A few of these training aids may be used carefully by amateurs, but others should never be tried by anyone except an experienced professional trainer.

1. Protective boots include those used for training and those allowed in shows. Rubber bell boots are regularly used in training any breed for any purpose. These boots serve to protect the heels or coronets of the front feet from over-reaching of the hind feet. We recommend bell boots for all training as a safeguard against injuries.

Quarter boots, which include the previously mentioned rubber bell boots, leather trotting boots (also known as "scalpers"), and leather hinged boots are traditional for five-gaited, fine harness, and roadster events. For show purposes, leather boots can be procured in several styles with added weight, serving the dual purpose of protection while encouraging higher action (fig. 55).

Warning: Some breed organizations do not allow added weight in boots, so check the rule book before showing.

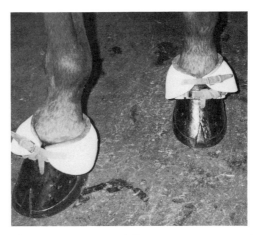

55. Protective boots come in many different shapes, sizes, and styles. Pictured here are hinged bell quarter boots.

2. Draw reins may be used in training by both riders and drivers. They provide leverage in helping to set the horse's head in a desired position, in addition to their use in attaining easier control. For the driving horse, the extended reins run from the driver's hands, forward through the terrets, through the bit rings, and back to be attached at the harness saddle (fig. 56). On the riding horse, draw reins can be used in two ways. The first, and less severe method is to have the extended reins run from the rider's hands, through the snaffle-bit rings, and back to be attached to the girth under the saddle flaps. The more severe fitting passes the reins from the rider's hand, through the bit rings, and then down between the horse's forelegs to be fastened to the girth.

Warning: Overuse of draw reins can cause the horse to learn to lean on the bit or become heavy in hand. They are best used by experienced horsemen, since draw reins used incorrectly may cause permanent problems.

3. Blinker hoods (blinder hoods), which come "open" or "closed," are often used and are routinely seen at shows. Open hoods keep the horse from seeing things other than what is in front of him so that he is not distracted by sights to the side or behind him. These are very useful in working the young colt, as he tends to pay more attention to the rider or driver without outside distractions (fig. 57).

120

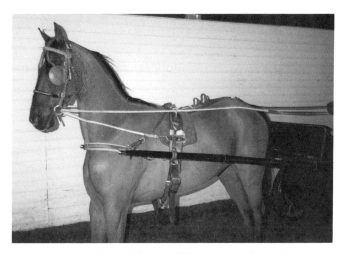

56. Extra leverage is obtained by use of draw reins, shown here.

57. Horse wearing a blinker hood.

Warning: *Closed* blinker hoods that totally obscure vision are dangerous, and we do not approve of their use by amateurs.

4. Chains, rattlers, or round leather straps (dog collars) are the most commonly used training aids for producing additional action and animation in show horses. They are placed around the pastern just above the hoof. Their purpose is to develop snappier movement of the legs as they tickle, jangle, or rattle with each step. While they are very effective on some horses, others, after an initial reaction, act as though they were not even there. If the horse does not respond as desired, there is no point in using them (figs. 58 & 59).

Warning: When using chains and rattlers, be certain to check the horse's pasterns and coronet bands regularly for signs of irritation.

5. Developers (also known as "stretchies" or "rubber bands") are the next step for those desiring to develop more or higher action. These devices are often incorrectly referred to as shackles but are very different and much less severe than true shackles, which will be discussed next. Developers are made by using two hobble straps, (placed around the front pasterns) and connected by surgical tubing. The tubing comes in various sizes, but one-half inch is most often used. The length depends on the length of leg of the horse and the

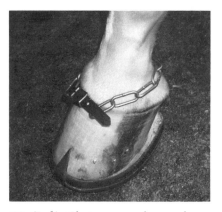 

58. (Left) Chains are used around pastern to encourage snappier movement.

59. (Right) Rattlers may also be used to produce additional action and balance.

desired motion. For a high, trappy trot, shorter connections are used. Developers should be used for only a few minutes at first. Then one can condition the horse to wear them longer, but not for more than ten minutes. Actually, five minutes should be ample to loosen a horse up as trainers often do just before a show class (fig. 60A & B).

Warning: Overuse of the developers may cause a horse to go higher in one leg than the other, to half lope, or to trot out of stride. Worst of all, overuse may cause injury to the muscular system. Also, be aware that the tubing may catch in the heel of the shoe, tripping the horse.

60A & B. Developers created from surgical tubing fastened to padded hobble straps (A). They enhance stride and action (B).

6. Shackles (used by some professionals) are the most drastic devices used for developing motion. These were known years ago as "running W's" and were used by horsemen to trip up a horse that might try to run away (fig. 61).

Warning: Shackles should not be used by an amateur as they can cause serious, permanent injury to a horse. Even when they are used by a professional, the horse may develop a lopsided trot.

Note: A word of caution. When showing, one should always check the rules applying to the artificial action devices mentioned

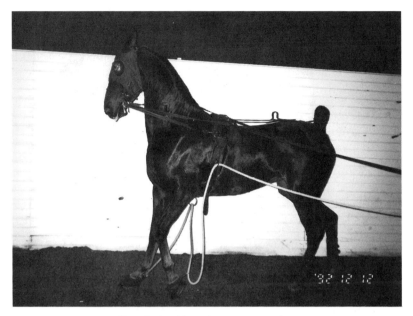

61. Horse moving off with shackles (also known as the running W).

above (chains, rattlers, developers, and shackles), since they may be different at each showground.

SHOW SHOEING

Although we discussed shoeing to some extent in Chapters 6 and 9, we are adding this section for those desiring a high action.

Generally, weighted shoes will help a horse move with more action. It is not unusual for show horses to be seen with five or even six inches of hoof, plus a pad, plus a shoe weighing from eighteen to thirty ounces. (A normal hoof is about four inches long, and a normal shoe weighs from twelve to sixteen ounces, depending on its size.) One may also see horses with their feet built up with pads to help attain the desired height. What may not be seen is lead added under or between pads to attain extra weight.

For horses requiring a long toe plus added weight, many trainers employ metal bands that run from the shoe up over the front of the hoof. The turnbuckle on the bands is tightened when showing and eased when the horse is at rest in the stall. These help prevent the horse's pulling the shoe with consequent loss of the extra hoof as well. Bands are also used on horses with brittle hoofs that do not hold the nails well (fig. 62).

Shoes may be procured from farriers or equestrian-supply catalogs as even-weight, toe-weight, or heel-weight. The toe-weight shoe may help to lengthen the stride or cause the horse to use its shoulders more. The heel-weight shoe tends to produce a trappier motion and thus is used on horses that are inclined to shoot the front legs forward rather than folding them up toward the elbow. It is not unusual to find the hind shoe with a "square" toe. Such a shoe is useful for the horse that interferes. Most show horses have a toe clip on the front shoe and clips on both sides of the hind shoes. The clips prevent the shoes from working back on the hoof. They are placed on both sides of the shoes on the horse's hind shoe so they do not interfere with the front feet.

A competent farrier is essential for the person desiring to enter show-horse divisions. Many farriers who are quite capable of shoeing driving, trail, or ordinary pleasure horses do not choose to enter the field of shoeing show horses. These farriers may be able to refer the reader to specialists in the field. Otherwise one may inquire at shows for the names of such blacksmiths.

Shoeing for maximum performance requires a lot of experimentation. Like people, horses respond in different ways to different kinds of shoes. As important as the shoes chosen (and sometimes

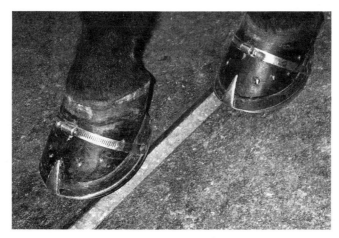

62. Bands with turnbuckles help to hold on heavy shoes with pads.

63. *A perfectly trained, high-actioned, fine harness horse being driven by a child. No action- or restrictive-training devices were used to train this horse, demonstrating that although many different devices are available, it is not necessary to use them.*

more important) is the angle of the hoof. The general rule is to follow the angle of the pastern. However, the angle of the hoof should never be less than forty-five degrees. To attain the best angle for some horses, heel pads or wedges are necessary.

After experimenting, one should finally shoe the horse with as little extra foot and weight as is satisfactory. Long hoofs and added weight induce problems that can become so serious as to cause permanent disability. The horse with normal hoof length and light shoes will last longer than one that carries a lot of foot and weight. We see many very young show horses that are overloaded, both with long hoofs and with heavy shoes. Their success today may mean a short career. The owner interested in his horse's welfare and ability to continue showing in the future will avoid placing any undue or excess stress on the horse.

Warning: When planning to show, one should check the American Horse Shows Association rules for specific shoeing regulations for different divisions and individual breeds.

CHAPTER 9

HINTS ON HORSE CARE

---•---

EXERCISING FACILITIES

Once a horse has been trained and shown, he can quite rightly expect to be allowed to relax a bit between shows—and most certainly between show seasons. He needs a chance to "be natural" after being kept on his toes for weeks or months of show-ring competition.

The best answer for the "broke" horse is to turn him out. This does not mean to simply take the saddle or harness off for the last time and immediately turn him loose in a field. However, the manner in which the horse is turned out will depend a great deal on the particular facilities available.

The ideal situation is the barn that opens into a paddock from the stall. With this arrangement an owner can keep the horse in or let him run in and out at will. This setup provides a warm place for the horse to return to if you decide to work him some winter's day. Both man and horse may then go through the cooling-out process in comparative comfort and without the danger of cold drafts on the horse.

The next best solution is a pasture with a three-sided shed for shelter. Here the horse may frolic as he pleases, yet still have a place to huddle away from wind, rain, or snow. Such sheds may be constructed with a large hayrack or hay manger so the horse can have access to feed for several days before the supply is replenished. The pasture must, of course, have water. Horses should have access to water at all times, so care must be taken to be sure that the supply does not freeze over in winter. Do not be fooled into thinking that a horse that eats snow is being sufficiently hydrated, because he is not! With this arrangement the amount of labor is negligible. Many horses will winter through in fine shape with just hay and water, but many others will require grain for good condition, so most owners feed their horses grain plus hay.

If given plenty to eat and drink and a good shelter outside, most will survive the rigors even of northern winters surprisingly well. However, if the owner happens to work the horse, he must be absolutely certain that he is thoroughly cooled out—his blood cool and his coat completely dry—before turning him back into the field.

When you first turn the horse out, limit his time outside to short periods for several days. This will accustom him to the new routine before he is left to his own devices. In addition, select a mild period in which to start the process. If the horse has been carrying long feet or heavy shoes, his feet will need special attention. They should be trimmed to a normal length and shod in light plates for protection. Horses that do not require long feet for showing may be allowed to run barefoot, depending on the terrain and the condition of their hoofs. If there is a question in your mind, you should consult a more experienced horseman or the blacksmith about hoof care for turn-out time.

The foregoing applies primarily to a finished horse that knows his lessons and will require but brief sessions to refresh his memory. For the green horse, you may prefer to continue light training during winter months, in a review fashion. Here the bitting harness is basic. The horse may be put in the bitting harness and allowed to exercise himself in the paddock, or he may be driven in long lines or longed. The bitting harness provides therapy for the mouth while allowing the horse to work without the weight of a rider or vehicle. Work in the bitting harness, in an enclosure large enough to let the horse hit a good stride yet small enough to ensure control for the trainer, can improve the stride and action along with the form and head-carriage of the horse.

Year-round exercise is vital for the horse. In the winter it is even more important, though people often let the horse stand in the stall

all week and then expect him to come out with perfect manners to drive or to ride on the weekend. Both for health reasons, which we'll mention later, and for safety reasons, which are obvious, be sure that the horse has some opportunity for daily exercise. The choice of exercise will depend on the facilities you have, the horse's needs, and the time you have to give.

BASIC STABLE CARE

It hardly seems necessary to emphasize that the horse's stall must be kept clean and dry. In most professional stables the stalls are thoroughly cleaned each morning and picked out later in the day. Cleaning the stall involves not only removing manure but also removing any moisture so the stall can be dry when bedded again.

There are many choices for footing in the stall, but most horsemen prefer a clay floor, packed on a good gravel and sand base for drainage. The clay forms a firm base that is not easily dug up by the horse's feet yet provides a good cushion and natural base. In some sections the native soil has enough clay in it to make a good natural footing in stalls.

As a second choice, a wood floor is the most popular. These floors rot out and do not provide the natural drainage and cushion advantages of a dirt floor, but where installed over a concrete base with good drainage system, they work very well. They can, of course, be swept clean.

Various masonry materials have been tried, from concrete to tar bases. Each of them has the advantage of being able to be swept clean, but each also has the disadvantage of being hard on the horse in getting up and down, and slippery to turn on. They are, therefore, undesirable. (Various new materials are always under experimentation; rubber matting affords good durability with some cushioning action, and may prove to be the perfect answer, for those who can afford it.)

The type of floor determines to some extent the type of bedding used. Straw is the all-time favorite for horsemen. If the horse is unblanketed a bed of straw will add gloss to his coat. (Some grooms make a wisp of straw into a grooming implement and use it to rub the horse dry or as a substitute for the currycomb.) The straw should be bright yellow, dry, and free of grass or foreign materials.

129

Other popular bedding materials are shavings and sawdust. Baled shavings are easier to store than sawdust and are always dry. Sawdust is sometimes damp to begin with and tends to mold, as well as having little drying effect in the stall. Where sawdust is available free or at a very slight cost, it may well be the choice, however. A manure fork, which works with straw, will not be useful with sawdust or shavings, which require a special fork; usually a shovel is necessary to complete the job. Some horses, particularly fat ones, which eat their bedding and are overfed, or horses with respiratory problems, do best on sawdust or shavings.

Those who clean out a stall will soon learn the most economical method of doing so, if they also happen to buy the bedding. After the stall is clean, add some fresh bedding to complete the job. It is not necessary to throw everything out of a stall every day; likewise, it is folly to ignore damp spots. Cleaning the stalls every day makes the chore easier and the stall healthier.

For the horse that is stabled and in training, a daily grooming is expected. All horses most certainly should be thoroughly cleaned after being worked, for the dust and dirt are best removed when the horse has been exercised and is warm. This leaves the horse happy from rub-down effects, and shining clean, thus easing the grooming for the next day.

Before going out to work, the horse should have at least a quick grooming. If you are pressed for time, start with a stiff brush and use it with quick, brisk motions, stroking to reach down to the dirt. Generally the brush should go in the direction of the hair, but a scrubbing motion may be used (with regard to the horse's reaction) on stubborn manure spots, such as hocks. A soft body brush stroked in the direction of the hair, is the next step. The final step is a towel or soft cloth, to polish him and remove the outside dust from the coat. Be sure to wipe off his head and around his eyes and his nostrils.

The mane and tail should be brushed with great care not to pull and break the hairs. For the show horse, which must carry a lush growth of mane and tail hair, it is best just to pick the straw and mats from them. Last, but probably most important, you must be sure to pick out his hooves and be sure they are clean, do not indicate thrush (which may be detected by a foul odor and soft mushy areas in the sole), and do not seem to be bruised or cut. Start cleaning the hoof with a hoof pick, beginning at the heel and working toward the toe.

Do not disturb the frog. All this is beneficial, both to the horse's health and in accustoming him to being handled.

While it is preferable to bring a horse in cool from work, if he comes in hot, he should be scraped and then rubbed with sacks or towels. Great care should be taken that he is not standing in a draft while you are rubbing him down. In very cold weather, it is wise to throw a cooler or sweatsheet on the horse, or at least a folded sheet or blanket over his back, covering his kidneys and quarters, to prevent a chill in these areas. If the weather permits, you may choose to give the horse a complete bath. Use warm (not hot) water, add a little liniment if you choose, wash him and scrape him thoroughly, and walk him cool under a cooler, sheet, or blanket. Too frequent bathing will remove the natural oils from the coat, so bathing should not be an everyday affair. Most stables recognize that there is no substitute for hard work to keep their horses shining and in top trim.

While you are walking the horse out, a few sips of water may be allowed at intervals, to take the edge from the horse's thirst and help him cool down. However, never allow a hot horse to drink his fill. All sorts of injuries may result, of which the worst may be a severe case of founder. The hotter he is, the longer it will take to properly cool him, and the less water he must be allowed to drink. When the horse is completely cooled out and has been carefully groomed, he may be turned loose in his stall, free to drink.

If you have been hauling a horse for several hours or longer, be sure to unload him and take him to a comfortable stall right away. Many people insist on walking a horse when the animal really needs to be turned loose in a stall so he may relieve the bladder. (Most horses do not want to wet in the trailer or van.) It is good policy to wait about a half hour after unloading a horse from a trip before watering or feeding. Just as water is prohibited to a hot horse, so is feed.

The amount and type of feed given a horse is a matter of personal preference and the needs of the individual horse. Certain horses will remain fat on two quarts of grain and some hay a day; others will require at least twelve quarts of grain and a sizable amount of hay. Oats are the basic grain for horses, but many good mixes are available, with bran, corn, molasses, and other fillers added. Vitamin and mineral supplements abound on the market. They are good but probably are not necessary for horses that have been raised on good pasture and feeds and are receiving adequate feed and mineralized salt supplies. One should be aware of local mineral deficiencies about which a veterinarian or an agricultural expert can advise.

The quality of hay determines how much of it a horse will need or want and also the amount of grain he will require. For example, properly cured, early cut green hay that includes a light mixture of legumes will provide more nutrients than straight timothy that is overripe. A horse will eat from ten to twenty pounds of hay a day, depending on the horse and the quality of the hay. Some horses prefer good hay to grain; others will eat more grain and go light on hay. There is no substitute for good hay, however, as it provides not only the nutrition the horse requires to stay healthy but bulk for his stomach and a soothing, relaxing, long meal.

When feeding it is best to water first, if there is no water in the stall; then provide hay; and last, give the grain ration. The horse should be watered again about an hour or more after feeding—not immediately afterward, which can cause the grain to wash into the stomach and ferment there, resulting in colic. Most stables feed hay morning and night and divide the grain ration into three feedings. Where this is not possible, the horse should be fed grain at least twice a day. Regularity in feeding schedule is more important than the hours chosen to feed. Whatever the hours, keep to them.

In feeding hay you can choose between a hay rack well up from the floor or a hay manger at floor level, or just throw loose hay in a corner of the stall. The hay manger prevents wastage and permits the horse to lower his head and eat in a natural manner. The hay rack, while having the disadvantage of dropping dust and seed into the eyes of the horse, is the choice for horses that are wearing tail sets and therefore find it difficult to reach down to eat off the ground.

If you have time it is good to shake up the bedding and straighten up the stall just before leaving for the night. Give the horse a good supply of hay to munch during the night, and he most certainly should be watered if you do not keep water in the stall.

In regard to watering, it is best for the horse to have water available at all time. It is handiest to have water cups in the stall so the horse can have water constantly without depending on man to carry it. Most horses will learn quickly to operate the automatic watering cups. However, these must be checked for cleanliness, as grain will fall into them from the animal's mouth. Further, since the horse should not have free access to water after he is worked, and if he must be turned into the stall for a moment, the cups must be shut off (or the bucket removed) before the horse drinks his fill. In cold weather, care must be taken that they do not freeze and the pipes burst.

Stable ventilation is essential, fresh air being vital to a clean, healthy stable and horse, but do be sure that no drafts are hitting the horse. Even a cool breeze in the summertime can be harmful to a hot horse.

Young horses that are turned out part of the year should be checked at least every three months for parasites and wormed accordingly. After horses have attained the age of five, and particularly if they are stabled most of the time, there is less danger of worm infestation, but worming at least twice a year is advisable. Adult horses that are turned out in paddocks or fields will need worming more often. However, if at any time older horses show loss of condition and dull coats, or rub their tails, a manure specimen should be taken to the veterinarian to be checked for worms. It is a good idea to have any horse checked out routinely by a veterinarian once a year at a time when the annual shots can be given.

Teeth will occasionally cause some trouble. If the horse becomes unusually irritable about the bits or exceptionally slow at eating, he may need the veterinarian. The vet will "float" or file down the offending sharp edges of the horse's teeth, which may be irritating the inside of his mouth. (Most problem mouths are caused by bad hands rather than bad teeth, however.)

SHOEING

Whether the horse is shod or not, his feet should be kept trimmed from the time he is a foal. Proper trimming is necessary for the healthy development of the foot and proper growth of the leg. In addition, skillful trimming by the farrier can improve or correct minor abnormalities of foot or limb position and way of moving. It is now common practice to shoe colts as yearlings, but it would be better for their feet if they were allowed to run barefoot, but trimmed, until at least three years old, permitting the hoof to grow unhindered to its full development. Early shoeing can cause undeveloped feet and the added danger of contracted heels.

133

Ideally, the toe of the foot should point exactly forward. If the colt is inclined to be splayfooted (toe out), the outside of the hoof should be trimmed down to encourage a straighter stance. Conversely, if the colt toes in, the inside of the foot should be trimmed. The angle between the front of the hoof and the ground should be no less than forty-five degrees and no more than fifty-five. Usually the hind feet stand at a higher angle than the front. The pastern angle has the determining effect upon the hoof angle. For dry, brittle feet, daily treatment with a good hoof dressing, pine tar, olive oil, or fish oil is recommended.

A barefoot horse should be trimmed every four to six weeks. Horses that are shod should be reset every six weeks, or eight at the most. The wall of the foot should be trimmed about level with the frog, and a rasp should be used to smooth the foot and level it. Shoes should follow the contour of the hoof and be about a quarter inch longer than the heel of the foot. See that your blacksmith is a man who takes care to make the shoes fit the horse, rather than the reverse. The description above of shoeing is merely a guide for the owner, to enable him to recognize whether the blacksmith is shoeing the horse correctly. Most owners should never attempt to shoe a horse; a good smith is highly trained and experienced, and the only person qualified to work on the horse's hoofs.

Forging is an annoying and painful habit, resulting more often from faulty shoeing than bad conformation or habits on the part of the horse. Forging is the striking of the hind feet against the front, causing the horse to cut the pasterns or coronets of the front feet. Though rolling the toe of the front shoe will often cause the horse to break more quickly in front, experimentation will show what method should be used to alleviate the problem. In any case, a good blacksmith should be able to cure the trouble. Putting bell boots on the horse's front feet will prevent cutting until the right solution is discovered.

With the show saddle horse, a very long foot and heavy weighted shoes are customary, whereas for many of the other breed classes, the rules limit the foot length. A long foot (say over four inches of toe) will help increase the action of the horse; weighted shoes do so, too. In general, toe weights cause a horse to reach further and thus to have more stride; heel weights tend to cause the horse to fold higher in his action. Veterinary authorities are opposed to extreme length of foot and excessive weight on the grounds that they impair agility, increase fatigue in the entire leg and foot, and precipitate hoof and limb unsoundnesses. Therefore, they always recommend the lightest shoe possible for the work to be done.

COMMON AILMENTS

Every stable should be equipped with alcohol, iodine, wound lotion, bandage cotton and bandages, liniment, hoof dressing, and a thermometer. The horse owner should know how to take the horse's temperature so that when the horse appears to be sick or in distress he may take this first step before calling the veterinarian. The owner should always summon professional help when trouble occurs and not try to diagnose an ailment by himself. The notes that follow are made only to acquaint the novice owner with the symptoms of the most common ailments.

Azoturia (Monday Morning Disease): This disease receives its nickname from the fact that it occurs apparently as a result of overfeeding and a lack of exercise, such as might occur if a horse is taken out to work on Monday after resting for several days (or even one day) in the stall and eating full rations. The horse seems to become paralyzed in his hindquarters, perspires profusely, and quivers all over. If this happens, try to return to the barn immediately. If you are some distance from home, find help, cover the horse with blankets, and try to keep him on his feet; if he gets down he may not be able to rise again. Send for a veterinarian immediately, as severe attacks can prove fatal.

Bowed Tendons: This results from severe strain or sprain to the tendons or ligaments behind the cannon bone. The horse will be very sensitive in the area of the bow and may even run a temperature. Rest is the best treatment, but the tendons may never go entirely back into line but leave a filled bow shape at the back of the leg. Horses may be perfectly sound for light work thereafter despite the bowed tendons.

Colic: The horse is restless, paws, lies down and rolls, and looks around at or bites his flanks in his discomfort. This is caused by indigestion. Try to keep the horse on his feet, walking him slowly, and give a dose of colic medicine if some is handy. If the discomfort persists after thirty minutes, call a veterinarian, as colic can become

135

complicated and death can result from an impacted bowel or twisted intestine.

Distemper (Shipping Fever): The horse has a high fever, accompanied by a discharge from the nostril that is watery at first and later becomes thick and yellow. The horse is depressed and has no appetite. He should be isolated and kept warm, his nostrils cleaned, and he should receive treatment as prescribed by a veterinarian. A complication is strangles, a swelling of the lower jaw, with infection in the glands, sometimes requiring opening of the infected area to drain off the pus.

Founder: A dreaded disease, founder may be caused by exhaustion, by concussion of sensitive parts of the foot, by failure to cool properly before feeding grain, or by watering while hot. The horse is lame, resting his weight to the back, with his forefeet extended. There may be heat in the hoof or hoofs, and a throbbing pulse may be felt by placing the thumb and middle finger around the pastern just above the coronet with the fingers at the back above the heel. The horse breathes heavily, is thirsty, and runs a high temperature. The veterinarian should be contacted immediately, for time is important in the administration of drugs that may affect the progress of the lameness. Meanwhile, soak the feet in hot water, which most veterinarians prefer to use today (the old remedy was cold water) and keep the body warm.

Navicular: Extremely long feet and heavy weight in shoes will predispose the horse to navicular, an injury to the navicular bone or tendons in the vicinity of the navicular joint. The horse points his toe and is sore, but may warm up and go sound. There is no cure, although the sensory nerve is sometimes removed surgically for temporary relief. The condition can also be alleviated with corrective shoeing, and the horse may stay sound if managed correctly.

Splint: Bony enlargements, usually found in the front leg between the inner splint bone and the cannon, are usually caused by overwork at an early age or by careless motion or a self-inflicted injury such as stamping at flies. They usually cause only temporary lameness and often disappear by themselves. Splints may be reduced by blistering or by rubbing with a strong liniment.

Tetanus: Commonly known as lockjaw, this infectious disease usually results from a puncture wound. The disease is characterized by spasms in the muscles of the head and neck, general rigidity, elevated tail, dilated nostrils, extended head. It is usually fatal. Horses should be routinely vaccinated against tetanus and given a booster by the veterinarian if it is recommended after an injury.

Thrush: A disease of the frog of the foot, thrush has a thick, dark discharge of foul odor. It is caused by filth and neglect of the feet. Clean the foot thoroughly and pack with finely ground bluestone. Other medications include equal parts of phenol and iodine, or cotton soaked in a ten to fifteen per cent sodium sulfapyridine solution. Good results may also be obtained by cleaning the foot thoroughly and washing with undiluted bleach. If thrush is caught early, lameness will soon disappear.

Lameness: Occasionally a horse will turn up lame in his stall or outside without evidence of any of the maladies mentioned above. Accidents happen in stalls—horses get "cast" against a wall and hurt themselves struggling to get up, or they may injure themselves just romping in the stall or when turned out. For most lamenesses the best cure is rest. Some horses will come out sound in a few days; others may require weeks of rest.

CHAPTER 10

CHOOSING YOUR HORSE

All kinds of rules have been laid down for the selection of a horse, from limericks about color to discussions of the angulation of every joint. The truth of the matter is that horses are like spouses—they come in all sizes, shapes, and dispositions, and the horse that perfectly suits one person might not be given stable-room by hundreds of other horse-lovers.

Nevertheless, certain basic principles must underlie the search for your horse. These principles will vary somewhat according to the age of the animals inspected (that is, from weanlings up), their breed, and their intended use.

The person who wants to train his horse may choose from those of weanling age up to age three, or sometimes even older, for there are still large breeders who have colts they don't get around to handling until the colts are mature. However, this is rare, and we must point out that a completely unbroken grown horse is ten times the gamble that a younger horse is. We have seen horses raised on the plains and untouched by humans that have been caught and sold to be broken as mature animals. Probably one in ten has made a satisfactory "using" horse; the others have either remained unbroken or have been added to the brood-mare ranks. On the other hand, many colts up to the age of two that were raised in this same wild manner have turned out very well, nine out of ten developing into tractable horses.

The more novice the prospective owner is, the younger the horse he selects should be. A weanling colt taken from his mother at the tender age of five months will happily adopt a human being who feeds and cares for him. A green amateur may take such a weanling and gradually develop a real comradeship, starting from the day when he is perhaps the bigger and stronger of the combination (and the smarter, too). At this stage the weanling can be physically mastered by the owner and psychologically befriended at the same time.

When the colt becomes a yearling, he has about seven hundred pounds of weight for you to contend with, and by the time he is two he may weigh a thousand pounds. So the odds against physical domination by the handler grow as the colt grows. The older the colt, or the later one starts his education, the more necessary superior knowledge on the part of the handler becomes, for no brute force can cope with a thousand-pound animal. From this point on the education must be done by the handler's brain, not his brawn.

Another advantage of the weanling for many buyers is their comparatively cheaper purchase price. It would be false to say that buying a weanling is always cheaper in the end than buying a started horse, but the initial investment for a weanling of a well-established breed may be several hundred, or even several thousand, dollars less than the price for a yearling or two-year-old of equal quality. Many people find it easier to pay the weanling price and then pay out the maintenance costs regularly than to fork out a larger cash sum for an older colt at the outset.

Sex is another price determinant. In many breeds a filly commands a much higher price than a stallion foal. On the other hand, a gelding, or a colt destined to be gelded, may be priced very reasonably. A fine stud colt to be gelded by yearling age is an excellent choice for the person who plans to spend years enjoying a reliable horse. Remember, it takes a high-quality stallion to become a high-quality gelding.

BREEDS

The choice of breed has a great influence on price ranges, so perhaps the starting point for the amateur horseman who wants to break and make his own horse is to decide what he really wants to do with the animal. For some people this is easy. Their aim is a family

64. Arabians excel at trail riding, as shown by this 1992 100-mile junior division winner in Vermont. Krista Blittersdorf on Rudie's Razzamatazz.

pet, to be trail ridden for pleasure only. For others the aim may be a family pet that can be shown at horse shows on weekends. From here on the choice becomes more difficult. Almost everyone who wants to break his own horse subconsciously wants a pet. But the further duties of the horse may become a maze of trail riding, tricks, hunting, horse shows, driving, or even dressage, eventually. When one views competitive fields as a long-term goal, the choice is most likely to come down to breeds that have been specially developed for achievements in that area. Let us consider the best-known breeds and their attributes for various assignments:

Thoroughbred: This is the breed that produces the great racing champions. For speed and endurance the Thoroughbred is supreme.

He is a big horse, ranging from 15.2 to 17 hands, and he is the choice of expert riders for hunt-seat riding, jumping, or dressage. As with all breeds, there are all kinds of temperaments, but it is recognized that the Thoroughbred may be "hot"; in short, he may be too sensitive, nervous, and high-strung for the novice or even average horse owner.

On the other hand, Thoroughbred crosses have produced top working hunters, dressage champions, and excellent endurance-ride horses; the mixture of outside blood often seems to "quiet" the hot blood of the Thoroughbred.

Arabian: Recognized as the oldest established breed of horses, and forerunner of the Thoroughbred and other breeds, the Arabian today still retains the original characteristics of the horse of the desert. He is classically pictured with a finely chiseled head, big eyes, a dish-face, flared nostrils, and a high natural tail carriage. Promoters of the Arabian have endeavored to retain his traditional qualities without any outcrossing, so his size has remained small to medium, ranging from 14 to 15.2 hands at the extremes. Fortunately, an even disposition has been emphasized, so that the Arabian, although pureblooded and running to the "hot" side, is still considered a tractable breed when handled with common sense. He is best suited to saddle work. He has proved his superiority in endurance and trail-ride competition, and does well on the range (fig. 64).

Morgan: America's own first established breed, the Morgan boasts many of the same qualities of the Arabian, including size and general type, although the Morgan may be heavier in weight and more substantial of limb. He is generally recognized as a "family horse," which can be played with all week and shown on Sunday, and has also adapted himself as a stylish harness horse and a working western horse without peer. He ranges from 14.1 to 15.1 hands generally and is a great weight-carrier. His gaits and bearing are appealing, both in harness and under saddle. Generally considered less "hot" than either the Thoroughbred or the Arabian, he is a current favorite in international driving competition. He has made great inroads in carriage driving and dressage (fig. 65).

American Saddlebred: Strictly an American breed developed primarily for show, this horse is without equal for beauty, refinement, adaptability, and heart. Like the Thoroughbred, some American Saddlebreds are considered too "hot" for novice horsemen, but they

141

are usually those most closely bred; many adapt themselves quietly to any situation. With Thoroughbred and Morgan blood most prominent in their ancestry, they usually range from 15 to 16 hands and have the bearing and action to make elegant entrants in harness or under saddle. They are most elegant in the show ring (fig. 66). They do not generally make endurance horses, although some have won in this field; occasionally, they have even made jumpers or cow ponies!

Hackney: While not usually mentioned among the favorite breeds, this group may offer excellent prospects for the person who wants a stylish, game horse or pony for harness or saddle. They are noted for their action, and only those who have ridden them appreciate the surprising smoothness of their high-actioned trot. Because they are looked upon as strictly show horses, prices on very nice youngsters that are not quite up to championship caliber are comparatively reasonable. However, they are not suitable for the long-distance trail rider or for western work, except parading.

National Show Horse: This is a relatively new breed comprising horses of mixed Arabian and American Saddlebred blood. The breed registry, founded in 1982, requires that the resulting offspring of Arabian and American Saddlebred matings have a minimum of twenty-five per cent Arabian blood in order to be eligible for registration. Breeders aim to produce versatile horses that possess the desirable qualities of both the Arabian and the American Saddlebred and are pretty, long-legged, long-necked, and athletic. As the name suggests, these horses are used primarily in the show ring.

Standardbred: The harness counterpart of the Thoroughbred, this highly developed American breed has produced world record after world record in harness racing, both trotting and pacing. Horses do not come any gamer than the Standardbred, but the years of emphasis on speed have sacrificed type and style so that now they appeal less to the eye as a breed than many others. Standardbreds often tend to be awkward at the canter or gallop. However, they are excellent choices for driving and may also be fine trail horses of excellent endurance. Their dispositions are good, and their size generally ranges from 15 to 16 hands.

Quarter Horse: This has become "the" western breed of the age, with a combination of blood flowing in its veins, including the Thoroughbred's. The Quarter Horse is a muscular, heavy individual

65. *A young rider works her Morgan on a country road. Even though she'll wear a saddle suit and derby when she shows, she wears protective headgear in practice.*

running from 14.3 to 15.1 hands and weighing up to thirteen hundred pounds. He has been specialized for western work or for quarter-mile racing and is without equal in these departments. He lacks style for park riding, however, and is totally deficient for harness work. Many have made excellent hunters. He is considered a quiet horse, tractable for novice or amateur horsemen.

Tennessee Walking Horse: Another American, developed in the South for plantation riding, this breed is one of the most praised and at the same time most maligned in our country. The specialized show Walkers have detracted from the Walker's former position as an ideal pleasure horse, but in truth the breed basically remains a quiet-dispositioned pleasure breed. The old-fashioned plantation horse was a joy to ride and very easy to get along with. They are not adaptable for harness and are generally not good in rough, mountainous terrain, but plantation Walking Horses may be excellent

143

66. American Saddlebred exhibitors aim for the perfection of Lover's Sensation, the epitome of the three-gaited show horse. She is shown by a master horseman, the late Earl Teater.

pleasure-riding and showing horses. However, they do not gait well for riding out with other breeds, so they are best used with other Walkers when out hacking.

These are the basic breeds from which you may choose your horse. We have not mentioned various imported breeds, strictly pony breeds, or the color breeds. When you consider a color breed, you should be aware of the combination of blood that may be offered.

DISPOSITION

The most important characteristic the amateur horseman needs in his colt is disposition, a trainable disposition. There are many kinds of tractable dispositions, from the very quiet to the highly nervous, but the first essential is that the colt is willing to learn. There are theories that blood is not important in rearing children and that environment is the all-important factor. If you believe this, apply it to humans only. Don't think that you can take any colt at all and get his cooperation through intelligent handling alone. Professional horsemen agree that dispositions and manners vary and that hardly any two horses can be handled in the same way.

There are plenty of problems in breaking horses to drive and ride without your having problems to start with. So give yourself a break, and look first for the colt with a disposition that complements your own. This will be different, of course, for different people. A capable, highly intelligent person with a maximum of self-control can take a highly nervous, wild-acting colt and produce a tractable, devoted pet in short order. On the other hand, we have seen complete novices, with little knowledge but lots of patience and a slow, quiet manner, achieve great success with colts considered too wild for any but the most expert professional. The secret to success in each case lies with the individual's suitability to the horse, and the colt's inherent trainability.

How can you tell anything about a wild colt, running out with a bunch of other colts? First, you may assume that the colt that comes up to the pasture fence, or up to people in the field, likes people and wants attention. This is a good sign. Second, notice the colt that advances cautiously, studies the situation, and shows great curiosity but never comes up or allows himself to be touched. Here is one that may be tractable, once he learns to trust his handler and becomes accustomed to human activity around him. You may see a "loner"— a colt that keeps to himself and associates with neither man nor beast. This type is to be avoided, for he dislikes his own kind and wants no part of cooperative activity. A colt that paces in the background, looking sullenly from side to side and daring anyone to block his path, is likely to have a resentful nature and to be distinctly uncooperative. Finally, there is the shy colt, which seems to want to come forward for attention but always gets driven back by the others. This type will often blossom under pampering and love but may remain timid in unusual situations.

Once you have observed the colt in the field, ask about the sire and dam. See them if possible, and find out what you can about their

145

personalities and abilities. A hot, silly mare is likely to produce the same; an unfriendly mare will try to instill this distrust of humans in her colt. About seventy-five per cent of a colt's disposition is likely to reflect his mother's, for she is the one who raised him and led him about during his first months of life.

Studying the head, and particularly the eyes, can tell you a lot about a colt's disposition. A large brown eye, prominently set, with thin eyelids and a mild but sensitive expression, usually indicates a naturally gentle horse. On the other hand, if the eye is large and prominent but shows too much white or is very dark in the center, and moves restlessly in the socket, a highly sensitive or flighty character may be suspected. Less common is a large, prominent, full eye partially covered by the eyelid or seen with eyes partly closed. This listless expression is common to the feline character, which may submit readily on one occasion and defy you completely the next.

Opposite to the trait of large eyes in varying forms is the small, round eye that is commonly called "pig-eye," especially when the dark part is surrounded by pink and perhaps eyelids showing pink. These small eyes set deep into the head usually show a sulky or unreliable disposition. Quite often the eye characteristics are compounded by narrowness between the eyes, a rounding or mulish nose, and ears that are set back, the head low between the ears.

In between the large, prominent, gentle, interested eye and the extreme pig-eye lie many variations of eye and head formation. Premiums are often paid for colts with beautiful, tiny heads—yet those with medium to large heads, complemented by large, expressively kind eyes, may well be the nicest animals to train and enjoy.

It is worth remembering that the time of year, weather, food, and housing can make a lot of difference in the looks of the green colt. Usually you will pay a premium for stock that is kept in fancy barns or paddocks and presented to you groomed and slick in every way, but a real gem may be hidden under long hair, mud, or a thin frame found on colts that are really "in the rough."

SUMMARY

Whatever colt you may choose should be vetted before the purchase is consummated. This is a protection to both buyer and seller. If you are purchasing a registered animal, be sure that the papers are in order and that you receive the papers, with a properly executed transfer of ownership, when you pay for the animal. You must expect to pay more for the registered animal than the unregistered, but usually buyers enjoy having papers to display whether or not they show or sell the animal later. We will sum up this chapter with these reminders:

1. Decide your goals for your colt—that is, decide what you want to do with him.
2. Decide which breeds or types are most likely to produce your goal.
3. Decide which age and sex will best suit your needs and pocketbook.
4. Contact breeders (lists may be obtained from most breed associations) to get a line on available stock and prices.
5. Go look at several possibilities before making a selection.
6. Try to see the sire and dam or get information on their backgrounds, especially their dispositions.
7. Choose the colt that seems to best complement your own personality and temperament.
8. Have the selection examined by a veterinarian or at least seen by a knowledgeable, experienced horseman in whom you have confidence.
9. If all the other steps have been followed satisfactorily, make your purchase and final arrangements for delivery. (While some breeders will arrange financing, the writers do not recommend long-term financing of a colt or horse.)
10. Be sure you have a halter on the colt and his papers in your hand, with proper transfer-of-ownership certificate included, when you pay for your purchase and take delivery.

CHAPTER 11

FINAL WORDS OF WISDOM

———————•———————

Throughout this book we have endeavored to provide clear and safe training methods for the amateur. In conclusion, we would like to offer the reader a few final words of wisdom. All too often we see people training and showing their horses without heeding what we feel are basic rules and procedures. Below are some of the commonsense practices we would like to see our readers follow:

GENERAL ADVICE

1. If you have purchased a colt (or even a mature horse) supposedly broke for a specific purpose, it is only prudent to proceed with caution. Go back to the basics as far as you think necessary to assure yourself that the horse is indeed broke and ready to be worked as you expected. It does not take long to put a bitting harness on, then drive in lines, to be sure that the horse is educated and responsive to the bit before one hitches or saddles to ride.

2. Every horse needs some exercise daily. With this in mind, remember that if he is not to be worked on certain days, at least he needs to be hand walked or turned out for some exercise.

3. Be sure that all tack is fitted properly before you begin working or

training. It is wise to move both harness- and saddle-horses after girthing them moderately. After the horse walks even just a minute, the saddle girth will need taking up again before you mount; the girth of the driving harness should also be checked. The horse should not be girthed so tightly as to be "cinch bound."

4. When working the horse, remember that a few minutes of positive training is better for progress than extended periods that may become tedious or boring. If you set a goal for your day's training and you achieve positive results in the first five minutes, quit. It is best to leave a good memory of the session with both the horse and yourself.

5. Be sure to cool the horse out properly. A hot horse should be covered with a cooler while being hand walked, even on hot days if there is any wind or a draft. Allow the colt only sips of water while walking out. If for any reason you cannot walk the horse, wrap him in a cooler and cross-tie him until he is dry.

6. Light bitting work is the best therapy one can use for curing mouth problems; it also avoids daily confrontations between handler and horse. Many top show horses have been kept "show ready" with exercise in the bitting harness ten or fifteen minutes a day, five days a week, with a ride or drive only once in the week. Some trainers rarely work their finished horses in the ring, instead seeking country lanes or training tracks to keep their horses fit and interested. These horses are fresh and ready to show.

7. Never pose the horse in an overstretched stance. Always teach the horse to stand so that its weight is over the front legs, which should be perpendicular to the ground. In some specific breeds for show the horse may stretch to this position with its hind legs slightly behind the perpendicular, but be careful not to encourage it to stretch too much. It is almost impossible to correct a horse that has learned to overstretch.

8. While a full-flowing tail is attractive, do not allow the horse's tail to grow so long that it drags on the ground when the horse is standing. A horse may react violently if he steps back on his tail.

149

9. Never run the draw reins through the curb bit ring, or use the running martingale on the curb rein.

SADDLE WORK ADVICE

10. Vary the horse's work routine.

a. Instead of starting off the work session circling left (counter-clockwise) in the ring, which is the normal way horses (except roadsters) enter a show ring, try circling to the right. Change the starting-off direction each day.

b. Vary the sequence of gaits rather than following the normal walk-trot-canter progression. With show horses, do continue to enter the ring at a trot so the horse associates "showing himself" right from the start. (This might not be applicable to some pleasure and western competitors.)

c. Once the horse nicely works the rail of the ring both ways at all gaits, try large circles at the trot and eventually at the canter. Also change direction by reversing diagonally across the ring, changing diagonals in the center at the trot, or changing leads in the center when cantering. All this work helps the horse to become more supple and more responsive.

d. Do not complete every workout with the canter. Change the final gait performed from day to day so the horse does not habitually associate cantering with the conclusion of a work session.

e. Avoid "lining up" routinely at the end of every work session. It is also wise to end your workout at various places in the ring. You might want to dismount at the far end of the ring and lead the horse if he has shown any sign of wanting to rush back to the barn.

11. If you are working a horse at the slow gait or rack, do not say "whoa" when he gets off beat. Seek control and balance through the reins while clucking and encouraging forward movement.

12. Be careful about disciplining the horse at the canter. Many colts are spoiled at the canter from over-correction. The basic truth is that you cannot fight a colt at the canter if you want to end up with a pleasant finished horse.

a. If the colt picks up the incorrect lead, don't jerk him to a halt to start over. Let him canter a few strides before calmly stopping him and then trying once again.

b. For the colt that has trouble getting off at the canter from the walk, try jogging or trotting him into it; be sure you are on the correct diagonal when pushing the colt into the canter.

c. Once the horse is trained and knows its leads by signals, it is usually the *rider's* fault if he picks up the wrong lead. Timing and feel are essential in the rider wanting to attain the correct lead each time.

d. The finished horse needs little work at the canter unless you are working toward a quiet lope for western pleasure.

HARNESS WORK ADVICE

13. Be sure that the harness is in good condition. A break in your harness can cause an accident that the horse will never forget. It is difficult to retrain a horse that has had a bad experience in harness; he is unlikely to be relaxed and dependable again.

14. If you are training the colt for driving, be sure to drive him in the lines for a few minutes first. You can then be sure he is comfortable with the fit of the harness before you put him between the shafts for hitching.

15. Be sure the check rein is not too tight. It should show some slack when the horse trots.

16. Be sure to have the horse well free of the cart before removing the harness bridle.

We hope this book proves valuable to whomever reads it. However, for the owner who runs into any trouble, we advise contacting a competent professional, sooner rather than later, to correct any problem before it gets out of hand. If you do decide to send your horse to a professional trainer, be sure to tell him the horse's complete history. In particular, tell him about the horse's problems and the difficulties you have encountered. This will save the trainer time and you extra expense.

APPENDIX

USEFUL ADDRESSES:

Breed and Show Associations:

American Horse Shows
  Association
220 East 42nd St. #409
New York, NY 10017-5876

American Hackney Horse
  Society
4059 Iron Works Pike
Building A
Lexington, KY 40511

American Morgan Horse
  Association
P.O. Box 960
Shelburne, VT 05482-0960

American Quarter Horse
  Association
P.O. Box 200
Amarillo, TX 79168-0001

American Saddlebred Horse
  Association
4093 Iron Works Pike
Lexington, KY 40511-8434

Arabian Horse Registry of
  America
12000 Zuni St.
Westminster, CO 80234-2300

The Jockey Club
(Thoroughbred)
821 Corporate Dr.
Lexington, KY 40503-2794

National Show Horse Registry
11700 Commonwealth Dr., #200
Louisville, KY 40299-2344

Tennessee Walking Horse
  Breeders' and Exhibitors'
  Association
P.O. Box 286
Lewisburg, TN 37091-0286

United States Trotting
  Association
(Standardbred)
750 Michigan Ave.
Columbus, OH 43215-1191

Show Horse Equipment Specialists:

Drury's Saddlery and Supplies
1638 Danville Rd.
Harrodsburg, KY 40330
800-541-2825

Fennell's Horse Supplies
Red Mile Rd.
Lexington, KY 40504
800-354-9087

LaSalle Harness Co.
221 Peeptoad Rd.
North Scituate, RI 02857
800-421-6069

National Bridle Shop Inc.
815 East Commerce
Lewisburg, TN 37091
800-251-3474

P & S Enterprises Inc.
24855 85th Ave.
Dixon, IA 52745
800-962-5057

Terry Bennett's Tack Inc.
Rt. 2, Box 598
Harrisonville, MO 64701
800-729-2816

World Champion Horse
   Equipment
P.O. Box 1007
Shelbyville, TN 37160
800-251-3490

General Equipment Suppliers:

Dover Saddlery
P.O. Box 5837
Holliston, MA 01746
800-989-1500

Eisers
360 Kiwanis Blvd.
Valmont Industrial Park
Hazelton, PA 18201-0096
800-526-6987

Libertyville Saddle Shop
P.O. Box M
Libertyville, IL 60048
800-872-3353

Millers
235 Murray Hill Parkway
East Rutherford, NJ 07073
800-553-7655

Schneiders
8255 Washington St.
Chagrin Falls, OH 44023
800-365-1311

State Line Tack
P.O. Box 1217
Plaistow, NH 03865
800-228-9208

Whitman Saddle Manufacturing
5272 West Michigan
Kalamazoo, MI 49006
800-253-0852

PHOTO CREDITS

INDEX

OTHER BOOKS FROM

TRAFALGAR SQUARE PUBLISHING

CARE OF THE STABLED HORSE
by David Hamer

CENTERED RIDING
by Sally Swift

DRIVING
An Instructional Guide to Driving Singles and Pairs
by Clive Richardson

FROM FOAL TO FULL GROWN
by Janet Lorch

LUNGEING THE HORSE AND RIDER
by Sheila Inderwick

OFF-CENTERED RIDING: OR NOT SO SWIFT
by Ruth Perkins, introduced by Sally Swift

RIDE WITH YOUR MIND
An Illustrated Masterclass in Right Brain Riding
by Mary Wanless

TALKING WITH HORSES
by Henry Blake

THAT WINNING FEELING!
A New Approach to Riding Using Psychocybernetics
by Jane Savoie

THINKING WITH HORSES
by Henry Blake

READER'S NOTES

READER'S NOTES

READER'S NOTES

READER'S NOTES

READER'S NOTES

636.1

Childs, Marilyn C.

Training your colt to ride
and drive